T0128209

THE
VALUE
OF YOUR IDEA$

Make Intellectual Property Work For You

Idea + Action = Success

EMMANUEL COFFY, MSEE, JD.

ALBERT DECADY, MSEE, MSIS, JD.

Emmanuel Coffy
COFFYLAW, LLC
515 Valley Street
Maplewood, NJ 07040
(800) 375-1804
info@coffylaw.com
www.coffylaw.com

Albert Decady
adecady@gmail.com
Twitter: @adecady

 www.trafford.com
North America & international
toll-free: 844-688-6899 (USA & Canada)
fax: 812 355 4082

CONTENTS

About The Authors ix
Preface xiii
Introduction.. xv

Chapter 1   Do I Have Ideas? 1
Chapter 2   What Is Intellectual Property (IP)? 17
Chapter 3   Patents.. 23
Chapter 4   Trademark... 27
Chapter 5   Copyright 33
Chapter 6   Trade Secret 39
Chapter 7   Internet/Website 43
Chapter 8   Traditional Knowledge 47
Chapter 9   Where Do I Secure My Intellectual Property? 51
Chapter 10   Do I Need an Attorney? 59
Chapter 11   Valuing Your Intellectual Property........................... 63
Chapter 12   Monetizing Your Intellectual Property 67
Chapter 13   Intellectual Property and the Courts 71
Chapter 14   Inventions that Have Shaped the 2010 Decade 75
Chapter 15   Inventions that Will Shape the Next 20 Years........... 79
Chapter 16   Conclusion.. 89

Appendix A   The Need for Signal Claims..................................... 91
Appendix B   List of Certain Organizations for Inventors 123
Appendix C   Resources.. 127
Appendix D   US Government Agencies.. 129
Index...131

DEDICATION

From A. Decady:

In loving memory of my father, Robes Decady.

This book is dedicated to my wife, Yandy; my daughters, Abigail and Lindsey; my son, Sebastian; my mother, Christiane Decady; my sisters, Marie Gesly Decady-Alexis, Tanyphla Decady Coulanges, and Carmelle Decady; my brother, Jean C. Decady; my nephews and nieces; all my uncles and aunts; all my cousins; all my family-and-laws; all friends; and all who have positively influenced my life.

From E. Coffy:

In loving memory of my parents Pierre Michel Rochener Coffy and Matina Michel whose sacrifices are beyond words.

This book is dedicated to my wife Suzie M. Coffy, RN, BSN, my adopted mother Oxane Charles to whom I owe a debt of gratitude, my daughter Catherine-Anne Coffy, my sons Akbar Coffy, MSEE, Adhlère Coffy, MSDS, MSUSI, Osvald-Emmanuel Coffy, my grandson Ahmad Coffy, my granddaughter Ayanah Coffy, my sisters: Chantal Coffy, RN, MD, Francoise Michel, RN, MD, and her husband Poncelet Michel, MD, Evelyne Coffy, RN, my brothers: Jean-Hiram Coffy, MSEE, Lamartiniere Coffy, MIS, MBA, Seymour Coffy, MD, my nephews and nieces, all my cousins, all friends and to all who have positively influenced my life.

ABOUT THE AUTHORS

Emmanuel Coffy is a registered patent attorney, and former patent examiner (www.coffylaw.com). Mr. Coffy is an inventor and had a long career as a digital design engineer. During his career as an engineer, he held positions such as lead design engineer. He supervised the US Air Force's largest network (Cape Canaveral–NASA) capable of supporting two simultaneous launches. His practice emphasizes patent application preparation, prosecution, and enforcement in the electronic arts, including business methods patents and design patents. Mr. Coffy has extensive experience in digital technologies, computer networks, and information technologies as well as device physics, which includes semiconductor applications. Mr. Coffy coinvented a device called the low friction apparatus issued as US Patent No. 8,585,092. He also has experience in reexamination, litigation support, patent infringement assessment, patentability opinion letters, cease-and-desist letters, demand letters, and due diligence. Mr. Coffy also advises clients on intellectual property strategy, licensing, trademark, trade secret, copyright, and related unfair competition/deceptive advertising issues. Mr. Coffy is the Co-host of the IP Breakfast podcast.

Practice Areas

Electrical/computer/software, telecommunications, mechanical, trademark and copyright, licensing, trade secrets and tech transfer, litigation and alternative dispute resolution infringement and validity analysis, trademark opposition/cancellation.

Admissions

Admitted to practice law in the state of New Jersey, the United States District Court of New Jersey, the US Court of Appeals for the Second Circuit, and the United States Patent and Trademark Office (USPTO).

Education

Juris Doctor (JD), Seton Hall University School of Law, Newark, New Jersey, 2003.

PhD, candidate in Technology Management, Stevens Institute of Technology, 1998–1999.

Master of Science in Electrical Engineering (MSEE), Florida Institute of Technology, Melbourne, Florida, 1993.

Bachelor of Science in Electrical Engineering (BSEE), Bridgeport Engineering Institute, Bridgeport, Connecticut, 1986.

Publications/Speeches/Presentations

"The need for signal claims" by Emmanuel Coffy and Albert Decady

The Best Presenter Award, November 2011 by HABNET

Congressional Certificate of Special Recognition by Hon. Yvette Clarke, November 2011

New York City Council Citation by Councilman Matthieu Eugene, November 2011

New York City Council Citation by Councilman Jumaane D. Williams, November 2011

Presentation at the World Camp Academy, New York, 2017.

Albert Decady is a seasoned senior official in the US Patent and Trademark Office (USPTO) with over twenty-seven years of experience in the field of intellectual property. Mr. Decady practiced patent law as an associate of the law firm of Sughrue and Mion, PLLC. He is currently a supervisory patent examiner at the USPTO.

Mr. Decady regularly serves as a media commentator and has lectured on intellectual property at the University of Maryland, College Park. He is the founder of the Haitian-American Lawyers Facebook group. He is also the founder and cohost of the IP Breakfast podcast. He was the founder and served as chairman of the Haitian-American Intellectual Property Association.

His academic credentials are extensive. Mr. Decady earned bachelor's and master's degrees in electrical engineering from the City College of New York, a master of science in information systems management from George Washington University, and a juris doctor from Washington College of Law American University. Public Leadership Credential, Harvard University, Harvard Kennedy School of Government. Mr. Decady studied abroad in London, England; Paris, France; Geneva, Switzerland; and Brussels, Belgium. Additionally, Mr. Decady is an active member of the Maryland Bar Association and the intellectual property section.

Decady resides in Maryland with his wife and three children and their canine Benji.

Admissions

Admitted to practice law in the state of Maryland, the Court of Appeal of Maryland, and the United States Patent and Trademark Office (USPTO).

Education

Juris Doctor, American University, Washington College of Law, Washington, DC, 2004

Juris Master, George Washington University/USPTO University

Master Management of Information System (MIS), George Washington University, 1998

Master of Electrical Engineering (MEE), City College of the City University of New York, 1992

Bachelor of Electrical Engineering (BEE), City College of the City University of New York, 1990

Publications/Speeches/Presentations

"The need for signal claims" by Emmanuel Coffy and Albert Decady

Who's who: American Law Students, 2004

Honorable mention, *Congressional Record*, vol. 162, no. 147, Hon. Frederica S. Wilson

PREFACE

I am honored to have been chosen by Mr. Emmanuel Coffy, Esq., and Mr. Albert Decady, Esq., to write the preface to their new book, *The Value of Your Idea$*.

I have had the honor and privilege of being Mr. Coffy's law partner for several years now. Both Mr. Coffy and Mr. Decady have written an important primer on how to use intellectual property law to protect one of your businesses' most important assets: its intellectual property.

Intellectual property takes many forms and a comprehensive knowledge of each form of protection for your intellectual property is imperative. If you attempt to try this on your own, you may risk and lose the value of all your hard work. History is filled with many examples of people who failed to properly protect their intellectual property, and the cost to them for the failure to do so is immeasurable.

The most notable example is someone people probably never heard of but whose idea is responsible for the vast majority of technological improvements in the world today, Vincent Cerf. Cerf is the codesigner of the TCP/IP protocols and the architecture of the internet.

The purpose of this book is to educate you on the types of intellectual property and how to utilize the appropriate method to keep your most valuable asset safe and to be able to realize the full value of your work, time, and effort. This book is also a motivational book inciting the reader to take action to bring about their ideas to reality. The book attempts to articulate in plain terms a subject matter that is complex and full of intricacies. The objective is to decipher for the layperson the different aspects of intellectual property, namely, its ideation to creation, its characterization, its capitalization, its materialization (implementation), its protection, its exploitation (commercialization), its monetization, and its valuation. To provide as much of a complete picture as possible, the book starts with a historical perspective of human creativity. Finally, the authors reduced the whole process to an equation: "idea + action = success." That is the theme of the book developed with maestria throughout.

I exhort you to take the time and make the effort to thoroughly read and understand the concepts in this book chapter by chapter. Once you have done so, I strongly urge you to take action and set up an initial strategy session with an IP professional so you know what is involved with the protection of your intellectual property.

Leonard R. Boyer, Esq.

INTRODUCTION

Everything is determined, the beginning as well as the end, by forces over which we have no control . . . we all dance to a mysterious tune, intoned in the distance by an invisible player.
—Albert Einstein.

An Overview of the History of Inventions throughout the Ages

Humankind's journey toward modernization has been and is long and incremental with each civilization contributing its efforts and ingenuity to making today's state of the art as we know it. No one civilization, country, tribe, community, or ethnic group can claim a monopoly on modernization. Rather, the advances or discoveries of one age, epoch, time period, or civilization are used as a building block to making what science is today, thereby reaping the benefits of past efforts. For example, according to the *Atlanta Black Star*, "[e]stimates supported by genetic, archaeological, paleontologic and other evidence, suggests that language probably emerged somewhere in Sub-Saharan Africa during the Middle Stone Age, hence the first words by humans were spoken by Africans." Another significant contribution by the Africans is the creation of the alphabet by the Carthaginians. Even globalization is not a product of today's commerce some may argue. History is not an exact science, and some historical facts are not reported with accuracy. Case in point, Christopher Columbus did not discover America as commonly known and reported because the land was inhabited when he arrived. There existed many flourishing civilizations on the continent. Be that as it may, history's knowledge base, however, is augmented and revised daily. This overview is certainly not a complete list of all the inventions the different civilizations have contributed.

We explore IP (intellectual property) in greater details later in the book. For now, let's contemplate how ideas (plus action) have changed the world. As it is said, "Past is prologue."

Mesopotamian Inventions (3500 BC–500 BC)

Mesopotamia is generally known as the first human civilization. Its origin dates so far back that there is no known evidence of any other civilized society before them. The original location of this civilization lies in the northeast by the Zagros Mountains, southeast by the Arabian Plateau. This geographic location is known today as Iraq, Syria, and Turkey. Mesopotamia is credited with the development of the idea of agriculture. They also started to domesticate animals for both food and to assist in farming.

Among its inventions are the wheel, the chariot, the sailboat, the plow, the discovery of time, astronomy and astrology, the map, mathematics, urbanization, the first form of writing (namely, cuneiform), agriculture, and irrigation.

Indus Valley Inventions (3300 BC–1900 BC)

Indus Valley civilization is widely recognized as one of the oldest civilizations. Its original location lies around the basin of the Indus River known today as northeast Afghanistan to Pakistan and northwest India. The Indu Valley civilization is also known as the Harappan civilization and the Mohenjo-Daro civilization, named after the excavation sites where the remains of the civilization were found.

Among its inventions are great accuracy in measuring length, mass, and time.

Egyptian Inventions (3150 BC–30 BC)

The Egyptian civilization lasted for about thirty centuries from its unification around 3100 BC to its conquest by Alexander the Great in 332 BC. It should be noted that Egypt is an African country located in the north of the continent of Africa. Egypt is known for its many monuments such as the great pyramids and other masterworks. Egypt was the preeminent civilization in the world. It relegates to the world a culture with few equals in the beauty of its art, the accomplishment of its architecture, or the richness of its religious traditions.[1] The ancient Egyptian civilization, a majestic civilization from the banks of the Nile, is known for its prodigious culture, its pharaohs, the enduring pyramids, and the Sphinx. It should be noted that Egypt was greatly influenced by the kingdom of Kush, also known as Nubia—today's Sudan.

Among its inventions are mathematics (2700 BC), calendar and clock, government, library, wine, cosmetics, mummification that preserves the ancient pharaohs to this day, medicine, hieroglyphs, and the great pyramids.

Ancient Greek Inventions (2700 BC–479 BC)

The Greek civilization is generally credited as being one of the most influential civilizations. The Greeks influenced Italy, Sicily, and North Africa and reached as far west as France. It's known today as Greece.

Among other things, the Greeks invented the ancient Olympics and formed the concept of democracy and the senate. They laid the foundations for modern geometry, biology, and physics and pioneered pozzolana (used with concrete).

Mayan Inventions (2600 BC–AD 900)

The ancient Mayan civilization flourished in Central America from about 2600 BC and is famous for having introduced the calendar.

---

[1] History.com.

The original location of this civilization lies in Yucatan known as the Yucatan, Quintana Roo, Campeche, Tabasco, and Chiapas in Mexico and south through Guatemala, Belize, El Salvador, and Honduras. The Mayans were gifted designers and architects who built grand structures including royal residences, galactic observatories, sanctuary pyramids, straight roads, and canals.[2]

Among its inventions are elastic (a long time before the process of vulcanization or rubber making), immense underground repositories to store water during the dry season, astronomy (the Mayans studied the heavenly bodies and recorded information on the development of the sun, the moon, Venus, and the stars), ball courts, chocolate, hallucinogenic drugs, law and order, mathematics, the Mayan calendar, the Mayan writing system (glyphs), and rubber.

Ancient Chinese Inventions (1600 BC–1046 BC)

The original location of the ancient Chinese civilization lies between the Yellow River and the Yangtze region. It's known today as the country of China. The ancient Chinese were very innovative. In meeting their daily needs, they innovatively created some of the most and long-lasting items in history. Ancient Chinese inventions date back to the Paleolithic period. The Chinese were always ahead of their contemporaries when it came to inventing valuable things. Their contribution to progress include four greatest inventions the world has known, namely, the compass, gunpowder, paper, and printing, to name a few. Below listed are the top 18 most famous Chinese inventions (including two from the medieval period):

Papermaking (AD 50–121), silk (202 BC–AD 220) during the Han Dynasty, tea production (AD 2737), kites, the seed drill (250 BC), deep drilling (second century BC), porcelain (1600 BC–1046 BC) during the Shang Dynasty, the compass, noodles, alcoholic beverages, iron and steel smelting, the wheelbarrow, acupuncture, the seismograph (AD 132), the Great Wall (260–210 BC), the Silk Road, gunpowder, and movable type printing.

---

[2] Ancienthistorylists.com.

Persian Inventions (550 BC–331 BC)

The original location of the Persian civilization covered Egypt in the west to Turkey in the north, through Mesopotamia to the Indus River in the east. The Persian civilization today is said to be geographically located in Iran. The Persian civilization is one of the most scientific civilizations of the ancient world due to its many inventions.

Among its inventions are the refrigerator (yakhchal), the battery, sulfuric acid, backgammon, alphabets, postal service, the concept of human rights, animation, taxation system, and water supply system (qanat).

Roman Inventions (550 BC–AD 465)

The original location or mass of land governed by the rulers during the Roman civilization was known as the village of Latini. In the present day, it is Italy, whose capital is Rome. The Roman civilization is said to be one of the most powerful civilizations to have existed. During its heyday, the Roman Empire ruled over a large mass of land. Its territory included present-day Mediterranean countries.

Among its inventions are the arches, grid-based cities, sewers and sanitation, roads and highways, aqueducts, Roman numerals, surgery tools and techniques, newspapers, and concrete. The Romans fully developed the potential of pozzolana.

Aztec Inventions (AD 1345–AD 1521)

The Aztec civilization occupied the territory located in the south central region of pre-Columbian Mexico. Today's Mexico is the epicenter of the Aztec civilization.

Among its inventions are popcorn, chocolate, chewing gum, and antispasmodic medication.

Incan Inventions (AD 1438–AD 1532)

The Incan civilization flourished in the area of Peru in Central America. Today the same territory comprises Ecuador, Peru, and Chile. The Incan was the largest empire in South America during the pre-Columbian era.

Among its inventions are roads, communications network, accounting system, terraces, freeze-drying, brain surgery, and rope bridges.

Inventions Still in Use Today

Algebra, music, maps, surgical instruments, flying machine, universities, camera, clocks, coffee—these inventions are attributable to the Muslims.

The stethoscope, pencil sharpener, hot air balloon, mayonnaise, braille, hairdryer, pasteurization, aqua lung, and the metric system are attributable to the French.

Inventions that Revolutionized the World

The wheel (3500 BC), compass (206 BC), waterwheel (50 BC), calendar (45 BC), pozzolana (concrete), clock (AD 725), printing press, steam engine (1712), vaccines (1796), steam-powered train (1814), electric battery (1800), computer (1822), refrigerator, telegraph (1830–1840), steel, electric bulb (1880), airplane (1903), transistors (1947), Arpanet (1969), iPod, GPS (global positioning satellite), microwave oven, calculator, radio, ATM, gun, telephone (including mobile phone), camera, television, automobile, artificial intelligence, and drone.

All these inventions are the products of someone's mind and idea brought to reality by perseverance and some ingenuity. These inventions have shaped the modern day. You may have noticed that many of these civilizations existed in parallel. This observation exemplifies the inventive character of human being. We are eternally condemned to use our creativity in search of a solution to our problems. Hence, we continually evolve if not physically but intellectually. As Einstein said, "Problems cannot be solved with the same mind that created them"; in other words, the same mind that created the problem cannot be the same that solves it. We have to escape or transcend the mindset that first created the problem in order to bring about a solution to the problem, and in the process, we evolve intellectually.

1 CHAPTER

DO I HAVE IDEAS?

The answer to this question is undoubtedly a yes for everyone. By definition, an idea is a thought or suggestion as to a possible course of action. But in this book, we are not referring to every thought or idea. Instead we will focus on ideas that, if acted upon, could become a book, a song, a play, a painting, a movie, a trademark, a patent, or the type of ideas that can create some commercial value. Even under this narrow definition of idea, we posit that we all have these ideas—ideas to create a new product, improve on a product, promote a product, create a business, come up with a play or a movie, etc. In the final analysis, we are all inventive.

But did you know that these ideas can make you rich? It is true. Well, ideas in and by themselves are not enough; you must couple the ideas with some consistent action. If for example you have an idea to create a certain machine, you must take steps to file for a patent, develop the machine, capitalize the project, put in place an intellectual property strategy, and commercialize the machine. If the idea is to write a recipe book, you must write the book. Ideas by themselves are not patentable, copyrightable, and may not be worth anything. However, an idea can be developed to be more.

Idea + Action

Here are some examples where ideas and action found synergy to be more.

★ ★ ★

There are a number of instances where people became rich by acting on simple ideas. These are just a few examples to illustrate the point.

Example A: The Moonwalk by Michael Jackson

You may be surprised to learn that Michael Jackson was an inventor. US Patent No. 5,255,452 was granted jointly to him and two of his costume-men on October 26, 1993. The patent described specially designed shoes that gave the illusion of leaning beyond his center of gravity. The move and associated gadget were created for his 1988 music video "Smooth Criminal."

In this example, monetary reward may not be readily evidenced by the success of the efforts expended in the pursuit of a certain idea. Michael probably did not sell one of these shoes. In this instance, Michael came up with a device to enable his performance of a move, namely, a dance that he thought about and choreographed. The success ultimately lies in the optimum performance of the move, which enhanced his popularity and therefore allowed him to make more money. Michael performed the moonwalk for the first time during his performance of "Billie Jean" on NBC's Motown twenty-fifth anniversary special celebrated on March 25, 1983. Although moonwalk may have originated with James Brown, moonwalk will forever be associated with Michael Jackson.

Of course, Michael Jackson had produced many albums and videos to which he owned the copyright, many world tours, and other acquired intellectual property rights (like the Beatles Catalog). According to *Money* magazine, in 2016 (partly due to that big catalog sale), the singer's estate pulled in $825 million, and his net *worth* was estimated to be about $500 million in 2017.[3]

Example B: Intermittent Car Windshield Wiper

Once, a man, Robert Kearns, retrofitted his car windshield wiper system to create what we now know today as the intermittent wiper.

---

[3] https://finance.yahoo.com/news/michael-jacksons-estate-worth-170000861.html.

His invention was later copied/infringed by Ford and Chrysler and perhaps other car manufacturers. He took them to court. It took many years to litigate, but his idea turn to millions of dollars:

In 1990, after more than a decade in the legal system, the Ford Motor Company agreed to settle with Robert Kearns for $10.2 million. In 1992, Kearns won a judgment against Chrysler for $30 million. Chrysler appealed the decision, but it was upheld when the U.S. Supreme Court refused to hear Chrysler's appeal.

His story was captured in the motion picture *Flash of Genius*, which continues to turn his idea to dollars.

Example C: The Super Soaker Water Gun

In another example, Lonnie Johnson invented one of the most successful toys of all time, the Super Soaker water gun (US Patent No. 5,878,914A). Yes, a water gun! Introduced in 1990, it has racked up retail sales of more than $1 billion. Yes, you read right, more than a billion dollars for a water gun toy.

★ ★ ★

Even failed ideas can turn out to be a good outcome. Something you may have started with even a poor idea, but while working on the idea, more ideas will come to your mind, thus improving your idea. And sometimes the starting idea leads to whole other things that are very useful. Case in point are the following:

Example D: Post-It Notes

In 1968, 3M's Spencer Silver was working on developing an ultrastrong adhesive for use in aircraft construction. Instead, a mistake led to the new adhesive called acrylate copolymer microspheres, which were a weak, pressure-sensitive adhesive. They had the unique characteristics of the microspheres being incredibly strong and resisting breaking and sticking at a tangent to the surface, which meant that the sticky substance could be peeled away without leaving residue and be reused. As of February 2018, 3M (the company that makes Post-it notes) estimated gross annual sales of more than $1 billion.

Yes! Not bad for an idea that did not work as it was intended by the inventor.

Example E: Pet Rock

Gary Dahl is the person behind this creation. The estimated profit is $15 million in just six months. The concept of selling a rock may be ridiculous. However, Gary Dahl figured out how to sell them and made millions in just several months.

He became a millionaire by selling rocks on a bed of hay for only $3.95. Every sale earned him about three dollars. Dahl sold rocks as hassle-free pets, which came with a cardboard box and pet training manual. These rocks became an instant hit and are one of the most successful fads of all time.

Now tell me that you could not come up with this idea. It requires no technical skills, just some marketing magic.

Example F: The Vanna White Case

In 1991, Vanna White, the well-known personality figure of *Wheel of Fortune*, filed suit in California's district court naming as defendants Samsung Electronics and David Deutsch Associates, which prepared an ad in 1988 depicting a robot dressed with a gown, jewelry, and wig to strongly resemble her likeness. The robot was dressed as a woman, turning letters like White does on *Wheel of Fortune*. Vanna White claimed that Samsung is enriching itself by profiting from her fame, fortune, and likeness without her express permission and without compensating her. After a long court battle, which made its way to the US Supreme Court, White was awarded more than $400,000 in damages. The Vanna White case is discussed in greater details in the "Rights of Publicity Section" on page 35.

Example G: Kim Kardashian West

On August 1, 2019, a federal district court in California awarded to Kimberly Noel Kardashian West (Kim Kardashian) a $2.7 million default judgment in her lawsuit against Misguided Inc. Kim

Kardashian is an American television personality and entrepreneur who garnered international fame for her personal life. Much of her life story was chronicled on the popular reality series *Keeping Up with the Kardashians*. In her lawsuit, she alleged that the fast fashion online retailer used her persona and likeness to sell its clothing. Said retailer repeatedly tagged her on Instagram and linked her to the retailer's e-commerce site. In her lawsuit against Misguide USA (Finance) Inc. and Misguided Limited, Kim accused the defendant of misappropriating her persona as part of its marketing and sales strategy to boost its sale of clothing online. Kim's complaint recited violations of her right of publicity, false designation of origin, and trademark infringement. Kim is also associated with Kimsaprincess Inc.

The district court granted a default judgment to the plaintiffs and awarded $2.7 million in damages to Kim. The court used a formula to come up with this amount. The court used nine unauthorized Instagram posts by Misguided at $300,000 per each post plus $59,600 in Attorney's fees, equating to the amount of approximately $2,759,600.

★ ★ ★

While many people do know that their ideas can be worth real money or even make them a millionaire, many people do not know how to go about moving from idea to reality. A great majority of people do not know how to protect their ideas and to generate money from such ideas. As shown above, most of the individuals described sought protection of their properties. In so doing, they no doubt went at great lengths to defend their ideas, including spending money in so doing.

It all starts with an idea, which usually means "a mental representational image of some object." Some may argue this definition is too narrow; idea is more than that. It may even extend to the inner core of human being to wit, the French philosopher Descartes exclaimed "cognito ergo sum," a literal translation of which is "I think, therefore I am." The byproduct of the thought process is that ideas are generated. To be materialized, an idea must be acted upon to thereby change the physical reality. Otherwise, the idea will remain in the abstract world, the graveyard of inactive thoughts, or dead ideas. To be relevant to the physical world, an idea must manifest its material existence within the space-time continuum. Interestingly, the abstract world is both the womb and the tomb of ideas: the former because that's where ideas originate, and the latter because that's where ideas that are not acted upon remain. Can an idea die? No, ideas do not die. In this context, we mean figuratively (the focal point or reference being you, the reader). Stated differently, your idea is abandoned due to your inaction and therefore, for all intents and purposes, that specific idea dies. A corollary to this question is if you thought of an idea and failed to act, can someone else think of the same idea? That's a subject for another book.

★ ★ ★

Idea + Action

An idea is just an idea, unless you turn it into something more. If you have an idea and you do not do anything with it, the idea is just an idea. No money will ever be generated by such an idea even if it was the best ideas since sliced bread. Therefore, the key to remember here is that you must take action to bring your ideas into reality and to extract the money out of it.

Although any ideas can generate money for you, not all ideas are afforded the same protection under the law. Those ideas that are offered special protection under the law make the set that is referred to as intellectual property (IP).

Who Owns My Ideas?

Hopefully you do. You would think that the question to this answer is simple, but it is not. For the most part, you own your ideas. But often, you do not own your ideas. This means that you have not taken the right step to secure a legal right to the idea. Not all ideas can be protected.

Your Ideas Already Owned by Another

An idea may be totally original to you, but it is already securely protected by someone else. Once protected by another person or entity, the idea becomes the property of that person or entity, and you may not be able to use it without proper permission or license. Therefore, it behooves an individual with an idea to be proactive. Why? Because two people may happen to think of the same idea at or about the same time. Whoever diligently takes the first step in materializing the idea may eventually own the idea by seeking the protection of the law. As a matter of fact, according to History-computer.com, "several people got the idea of a microprocessor at the same time, but only one got the all glory and he was the engineer Ted Hoff (together with co-inventor Mazor and Faggin) at Intel Corp., based in Santa Clara, California." Further, still according to History-computer.com, "[i]n 1990, another U.S. engineer and inventor-Gilbert Hyatt from Los Angeles, after a 20-year battle with the U.S. Patent Office, announced that he had finally received a certificate of intellectual ownership of a single-chip microprocessor that he says he invented in 1968, at least a year before Intel started (see U.S. patent 4942516)." We can all learn from these anecdotes.

Your Ideas May Belong to Your Employer

Many people sign a contract as a condition for employment. These types of contracts often have clauses in them that give the employer the right to all ideas or inventions that are born in the mind of an employee during that employment. This situation arises when an employee's signs a kind of contract, i.e., employment contract or work for hire. Whether the invention belongs to your employer all depends on the terms of the contract that you sign. So before you take your next job or gig work, you may want to take time to carefully read the employment contract.

For example, if you are hired to create software or an app for tracking all persons who have come in contact with a patient who recently tested positive for coronavirus, the employer may own all algorithms developed to make the software work. So if you later find other usage for those algorithm or the whole software, for example, to trace a murder using the same type of data and algorithm, you may find that you don't own this idea anymore and that you gave it up as part of the contract.

However, if the idea that you develop in your own time, with your own resources, and is not subject to the contract, then you may still own the idea. From the previous example, if you now develop a software or app to allow small businesses to track sales. Assuming that is also not part of the contract, then you may still own this idea.

Whether the idea belongs to you is a complex question. The right answer is, really, it depends. You may or may not own the idea. We say it depends because like many things in law, the actual facts surrounding the situation are important, and different facts can yield different results. That is one reason we advocate that you consult with a lawyer who could examine the particular circumstances and advise you accordingly on the best course of action.

Could My Ideas Be Protected?

Assuming that you have not given away your rights to your ideas, most of your ideas can be protected under one scheme of the law or another. Sometimes it is sufficient to protect your idea under only one of the schemes, but in other situations, it is best to protect your idea under several of these schemes. This is the idea of getting a bundle of rights to protect your ideas.

Many products out on the market are covered under several schemes of intellectual property, for example, patent and trademark. The patent protects a design, plant variety, process, machine, article of manufacture, a compound. For example, the compound formula $C_8H_9NO_2$, which is known as acetaminophen, was protected by patent(s). These patents are now expired. Patents, you will find out, do have an expiration date, which is twenty years from filing. (In fact, many of the patents expired seventeen years from issue—there was a law change that we are not going to discuss in this book.)

This formula, $C_8H_9NO_2$, which is known as acetaminophen, may not mean anything to you, but it is an item that you are very familiar with by its trade name: Tylenol. This is an example of a trademark.

While the patent has expired and that any company with the capability to manufacture generic medicine can produce acetaminophen, the company was able to keep its market share because of the trademark. In fact, there are many generics on the market. However, the trademark is still in force, and thus the company who has the mark can still continue to generate revenue. There is no expiration date for a trademark. Therefore, if you have a good trademark, one that consumers like to buy, you can sell them forever and a day. This is why you want to protect your idea with a bundle of rights—here with a patent and a trademark. The patent allowed the owner to exclude all others from manufacturing the product for the time period the patent is in force while the product owner is promoting the brand. After the patent expired, the brand is well-known and will continue to protect the market share.

★ ★ ★

Ideas + Action = Success

In the previous section, we provided examples of ideas that were acted upon by their owner and have been very successful. Remember, an idea by itself will not lead to success. When confronted by a problem, we can all summon our intellect to the rescue, and ideas will be generated. However, we cannot emphasize any more than to just repeat ad nauseam that you must take action, protect your idea, and take some additional steps, like marketing. It is all these steps cumulatively that will lead to success.

Action

By action, we mean that you must take concrete steps to make your idea a reality. If your idea is to write a book, you must start writing; if it is an idea to build a machine, start drawing it so it can start to have form, and continue to develop your concept. This is referred to as the idea-stage startup. Lately, there has been an effort in the industry to standardize the process starting with an idea to bringing a product or service to market. Many idea-stage startups may not develop to further stages. Some will evolve to the next stages, namely, pre-seed and seed stage, the established stage, the enforcement stage, and the mature stage. Each stage requires specific actions in order to advance to the next. At this stage where a product is contemplated, the startup has entered the pre-seed and seed stage. At this stage, where some professional services will be sought, then some funds are needed. You, the founder, need to step up to the plate to raise some funds as part of the action referred to above. You may have to reach out to family and friends to raise the necessary funds. Investor Guide reported that this form of personal fundraising accounts for over $60 billion per year.[4] Although not recommended, if you decide to proceed without the services of a legal professional, you need to know when to protect your idea with an NDA (nondisclosure agreement) in dealing with certain service providers. Next, if the idea is to build a machine, take notes on how it will work and diligently work on the project to build a prototype. You can also start writing your application for patent (see the Manual of Patent and Procedure cited in the references). Seek consultation with IP lawyers to create a plan. Start to build a budget to pay for professional services that you may need to help you protect your intellectual property rights. The price may vary depending on the service and who is doing the work, so do your due diligence. Having raised some funds from personal asset, family, and friends, your startup enters the pre-seed stage, which is a term investors call startups seeking funding in the range of $750,000 or less.[5] Having built a prototype of the machine and performed some tests, making some modifications to the original idea, then the startup moves to the seed stage financing. In this stage, your startup could raise several million dollars from funders who typically invest up to $1 million each. From the seed stage, the startup moves to the established stage. It may take years before achieving this milestone. Financing at this stage is done through series A, series B, series C rounds, and additional rounds. Having launched the product or making the service available to the public, competitors may infringe your IP rights. You now need to enforce your rights because intellectual property is not self-enforcing; thus, the enforcement stage. With so much investment at stake, some action must be taken to protect the investment, which

---

[4] Investor Guide: Types of Investors, Fundable (2014), https://www.fundable.com/learn/resources/guides/investor-guide/types-of-investors.

[5] Rob Go, what are Pre-Seed Rounds and Why Do They Exist? Next View Ventures Blog (Jan 26, 2016) https://nextviewventures.com/blog/what-are-pre-seed-rounds/

may include litigation. Finally, having survived the enforcement stage, the startup is said to be mature.

Not every startup follows the above route, some may use crowdfunding[6] or opt to self-finance using whatever means the founder has at his/her disposal. For example, one may choose to remortgage the house, use credit cards, withdraw from saving accounts, and the like. This route is referred to as bootstrapping. This way, the founder retains full ownership and therefore full control of the company.

Of course, if your idea is a trademark, you will need to file for a trademark or start using your mark in commerce.

Success

Success is not just defined here in the amount of money made. Of course, money is a good metric, but not the only measure. Sometimes success is to take steps to bring about your idea to reality. We are doing just that here by writing this book. It was a long-time idea that we are bringing to reality. We will define success by publishing this book, and if we are so lucky to have changed the life of one of our readers that, but for this book, have taken action on an idea—that is success.

Note that in some industries, success will take time to show its head. It is like a good wine; you cannot get it in a short time. So you must be patient and be consistent and persevere; your day will come. Many artists don't ever know the full success of their work, for the value of their works often are more valuable after their passing than when they are alive. We can cite a number of examples, but suffice it to mention the well-known painting *Mona Lisa* by Leonardo da Vinci and visual arts by the French Impressionist Oscar-Claude Monet.

---

[6] Crowdfunding is the practice of funding a project or venture by raising many small amounts of money from a large number of people, typically via the Internet. "Musicians, filmmakers, and artists have successfully raised funds and fostered awareness through crowdfunding"

Commercialization

Having implemented the idea and capitalized the enterprise, the next action is to commercialize the product or service. Simply, a product or service is commercialized by introducing it to the market. Access to the market is an important element in the overall competitiveness equation. To access a market and secure a stable and predictable market share is a major challenge facing most SMEs. In addition to patents and trade secrets, the proper use and protection of trademarks and industrial designs by an SME could provide it the much-needed competitive advantage.[7] The document further indicates "[c]ustomers should be able to distinguish, at a glance, between your products or services and those of your competitors and associate them with certain desired qualities. Intellectual property, when efficiently used, is an important tool in creating an image for your business in the minds of your current and potential customers and in positioning your business in the market. IP rights, combined with other marketing tools (such as advertisements and other sales promotion activities) are crucial for: (a) Differentiating your products and services and making them easily recognizable; (b) Promoting your products or services and creating a loyal clientele; (c) Diversifying your market strategy to various target groups; (d) Marketing your products or services in foreign countries." There are different options available to bring a product to market. We will briefly outline a few of these options. However, the reader should consult a marketing professional or look for a reference dedicated to marketing a new product or service.

The options most professionals in the field suggest are (a) direct sales, (b) sales representative, (c) franchising, (d) distribution, (e) joint venture, and (f) licensing.

Direct Sales

Under this option, the intellectual property owner handles all aspects of the business, including the marketing and sales of the product. Manufacturing may very well be outsourced because the intellectual property owner most likely lacks the wherewithal to

---

[7] WIPO—IP Management and Commercialization of New Products, p. 26, 105.

undertake such an endeavor. A majority of marketing professionals agree that a new startup would most likely find it difficult to hire people with the knowledge and ability to market and sell the product. However, the benefit of this option is that the owner has not made a commitment to another party, so the owner may change direction at any time and pursue another commercialization strategy.

Sales Representative

Sales representative involves outsourcing sales to outside sales representatives. Generally, this arrangement involves a sales representative who will take orders, which may be accepted or rejected by the company. If accepted, the sales representative will then obtain a commission of 5, 10, or 15 percent of sales or some other percentage agreed by the parties. While 10 percent is common, the commission rate will depend on the industry and the person involved. For the company, the benefit is that it typically pays commissions out of money already received, so there's no advance investment.

Franchising

Franchising is mainly a creature of state law and is a highly regulated area. However, antitrust law, which is federal law, may affect this area of business. Another area of federal law having some impact on a franchise is trademark. A franchisor would most likely have a trademark that identifies the source of the product and the qualities associated with the product. A consumer would expect the same quality wherever that mark is used. If a company tries to impose a lot of marketing obligations on its franchisee, Federal Trade Commission (FTC) may intervene.

Distribution

In a distribution arrangement, an owner sells his/her product to a third-party distributor, who resells it to other people. Once the distributor takes ownership of the product, some risks are attached to the transfer.

Common distribution agreements include OEM (original equipment manufacturer) agreements where the distributor will include the OEM product as part of its offering or in a bundle with other products and VAR (value added reseller) agreements where the distributor will integrate the manufacturer's product with its own services.

Private label agreements are arrangements where the manufacturer will produce its own product, but with the distributor's branding.

Joint Venture

In a joint venture arrangement, the intellectual property owner licenses his/her intellectual property to another party while holding an ownership interest in the intellectual property. A joint venture is a separate entity where an owner may receive money both from owning the entity and from royalties. The risk is that a joint venture may have a different corporate culture and goal than the intellectual property owner. The benefit is that such an arrangement may potentially shield the intellectual property owner from some liability.

Licensing

You can make money for an IP that you own. For example, if you have an idea to create a machine, you can patent it as an invention. If you are granted the patent by the USPTO, then you can make the product or simply license it to another company to make the product and pay you a royalty. The bundle of rights referred to above includes licensing and assignment. Licensing in, many cases, the preferred form of exploitation of a particular IP asset. Generally, there are three types of licenses, namely, (1) express license; (2) implied license and (3) compulsory license. Most IP can be licensed. Some examples include music licensing, dramatic performance licensing, software licensing, etc. Detailed discussion about these licenses are beyond the scope of this book.

In a license, the technology owner and the licensee divides the future economic benefit according to the terms of a license. The rights are divided and the relative risks to be borne by the licensor and licensee determine how the economic benefit will be shared. The licensee typically pays for these rights in the form of royalty. Companies also often engage in cross-licensing by exchanging access to specified technologies within their respective portfolios. Cross-licensing often results when companies are trying to fend off infringement suits.

In the context of licensing, although different methods of valuation are used in practice, the income approach is the preferred method. This method estimates the economic benefit of the licensee, considers the parties' relative risks, considers the costs of exploitation and who will bear them, and calculates the present value of the benefit to which the licensor is entitled. Each of the methods are being used in the industry as methods for arriving at a particular royalty. The reader should note each of these methods have their own shortcomings.

Technology Sale

The sale of intellectual property is not seen very often, except for the sale of a product line or the transfer of a business. In certain cases, an exclusive license is preferred. For example, if the intellectual property owner will be receiving an ongoing payment for the sale, then it is recommended that the owner offer an exclusive license. As such, the owner will have a better chance of reclaiming the intellectual property if the buyer fails to make future payments to the owner.

To conclude, the reader is advised that the selection of the optimal commercialization strategy depends on several factors, e.g., the nature of the product, the industry, and the availability of financing, with different arrangements being appropriate for different areas.

★ ★ ★

You Must Have Faith in Your Idea

Faith is believing in yourself even if no one does.

A million tries should not stop you from achieving your end result. Too often, people give up before they achieve their end goal. This may be a result of the instantaneous life that we live today. We can get almost anything in an instant: we eat instant food, or cooked food is delivered almost instantly by pressing a button on an app in our handheld device; our ride is simply a click away, and all our purchases seem to magically show up at our doorstep in less than twenty-four hours and shrinking soon to be less than two hours. All great inventions that took a long time to develop, but could give us the wrong perception of the work it took to make them happen. You will need to understand that success in developing your idea is not a quick rich scheme, and it may take several tries before you get it right. You might even think that you are failing or you have failed even a few times. If this is any consolation, note that oftentimes, corporations keep secret the number and nature of failures experienced in developing a product. That is because failures may actually have some value hidden within. At the very least, you know what does not work. Success is the result of overcoming your failures, and each time you fail, you would have learned yet one more way that your invention does not work. And after a thousand and nth time, when you get it right because you did not give up, there it is—success!

There will be times that you want to give up. We want you to remember each time you have such a feeling of failure, defeat, or giving up, that it took Thomas Edison and his associates two years, between 1878 to 1880, *and* at least three *thousand* different theories/ tries to develop an efficient incandescent lamp before they could find one that worked. So it pays to stay on task, have faith, and persevere. Your effort will not be in vain.

2 CHAPTER

WHAT IS INTELLECTUAL PROPERTY (IP)?

Intellectual property (IP) is the fruit of your mind—your ideas. (The Oxford dictionary defines IP as "a work or invention that is the result of creativity, such as a manuscript or a design, to which one has rights and for which one may apply for a patent, copyright, trademark, etc.") Intellectual property (IP) refers to creations of the mind, such as inventions, literary and artistic works, designs, and symbols, names, and images used in commerce.[8] Everyone has them in abundance. Everyone is capable of great ideas. By everyone, I mean the rich and the poor, the educated and uneducated, old and young, even the youngest of children have ideas—all these ideas, no matter from whose brain they were born, if nurtured properly can have great potential to turn into something bigger than an idea. All these ideas can be materialized and turned into money. We all need to be familiar with IP, whatever your field of endeavor, because it is so ubiquitous in today's world.

Caution: Truth be told, not all ideas are great ideas nor are will all ideas make you money. For example, ideas that would result in illegal activities do not fall in the set of good ideas in the context of this book, even if such ideas do sometimes generate money. Stay clear of all illegal activities; you will live to enjoy the fruit of your labor.

Myth

There are many people who think that intellectual property belongs to only a certain group of people, like the educated. For

---
[8] https://www.wipo.int/about-ip/en/.

example, some believe that only engineers, physicists, computer scientists, chemists, or others possessing such high knowledge of their subject are worthy of being inventors. This is a myth. Although many inventors are scientists with high degrees bestowed onto them, an inventor does not have to have a degree in anything to be an inventor.

Evolution of Intellectual Property

Although early civilizations have all invented, history, however, lacks any concrete evidence of the mechanism used to legally protect these inventions. Some of these early civilizations were nevertheless known for their law-and-order system. In all likelihood, the modern concept of intellectual property developed in England in the seventeenth and eighteenth centuries. In the nineteenth century, the term *intellectual property* was somewhat used, whereas intellectual property became commonplace in the majority of the world's legal system in the twentieth century. The major and well-known legislation was the Statute of Monopolies (1624), which embodied the patent laws. Another legislation, namely, the Statute of Anne (1710), is credited as having originated the copyright law.

Intellectual property is divided into three main categories. (1) Industrial property includes inventions (patents), trademarks, industrial designs, and geographic indications of source; (2) copyright includes literary and artistic works such as novels, poems and plays, films, musical works, artistic works (drawings, paintings, photographs, and sculptures), and architectural designs. Rights related to copyright include those of performing artists in their performances, producers of phonograms in their recordings, and those of broadcasters in their radio and television program.[1] (3) Traditional knowledge,[9] indigenous knowledge, and local knowledge, generally refer to knowledge systems embedded in the cultural tradition, regional, indigenous, or local communities. Traditional knowledge includes types of knowledge about traditional technologies of subsistence (e.g., tools and techniques for hunting or agriculture), midwifery, ethnobotany and ecological knowledge, traditional medicine, celestial navigation, ethno-astronomy, climate, and others. These kinds of knowledge, crucial

---

[9] See Wikipedia.

for subsistence and survival, are generally based on accumulations of empirical observation and on interaction with the environment.

The concept of intellectual property, most notably patent, trademark, copyright, and licensing, was always known in certain circles. Businesses and business owners have been making use of these tools for centuries now to protect and develop their businesses. However, the knowledge of these subjects are not commonplace in the general public. Hence, this book attempts to articulate in plain terms a subject matter that is complex and full of intricacies. The objective is to decipher for the layperson the different aspects of intellectual property, namely, its ideation to creation, its characterization, its capitalization, its materialization (implementation), its protection, exploitation (commercialization), and its valuation—to provide as much of a complete picture as possible such that the entrepreneur can become acquainted with the different aspects of intellectual property and the language associated with it. As we can all appreciate, every industry, every profession, and any social endeavor has its own lingo.

In the past, there were a number of television (TV) shows like *American Inventor* and *Big Ideas*, to name a few, that try to make such information mainstream. However, these TV programs only scratch the surface of the subject and do not offer the details necessary for a person to fully appreciate and use intellectual property to their benefits. Like they say, the devil is in the details, which these TV programs do not start to tackle for the viewers.

Like everything else, an interested person can use the internet to find out the needed information. There are many dedicated websites to intellectual property, for example, the official website of the United States Patent and Trademark Office (www.uspto.gov) or the website of the World Intellectual Property Organization (www.wipo.org) and many others (a part list can be found in the resource page in the back on this book). One can use these websites as a starting point to learn about the subject of intellectual property. However, navigating through the maze of information offered by the internet may prove to be a formidable exercise in research, which may lead to information overload. This book sought to make the information simple and easy to digest. This book can be used as a quick reference guide, while other resources can be used for more in-depth knowledge of the subject. The goal of this book is to inform the reader about the tools used in intellectual property and to provide the reader with the knowledge necessary to take advantage of these tools and to prosper from their ideas.

IP Now

IP is the commodity and currency of the information age (the twenty-first century). For example, in 2016, intellectual property asset transactions accounted for more than 20 percent of world trade, or approximately US$740 billion. Compared to this amount today, just in the United States, 52 percent of all US merchandise exports is IP based or approximately $6.6 trillion dollars (38.2 percent of GDP). In the midseventies, tangible assets made up approximately 80 percent of a company's value, with the remaining 20 percent in intangible assets. Today, intangible assets make up 84 percent of the value of a company, and only 16 percent make up the tangible assets.

The rapid growth of IP coincides with the emergence of the digital economy, with the five largest companies by market cap changing too. In 1975, they were IBM, Exxon Mobil, P&G, GE, and 3M. In 2018, they are Apple, Alphabet, Microsoft, Amazon, and Facebook. Explosion of smart devices grew from 15 billion in 2015 to 200 billion in 2020 during that period.

Types of IP

- Patents (process, machine, article of manufacture, composition of matter, designs, plants)
- Copyrights (work of authorship fixed in tangible medium)
- Trademarks (sound, device, symbol, word, phrase, brand name)
- Trade secrets (process, know-how, recipe)
- Trade dress (various elements used to promote a product)
- Databases, customer lists
- Video/audiovisual material
- B2B rights (use rights, broadcast rights, marketing rights, franchise agreements, royalty agreements, licensing agreements, sponsorship agreements, mortgage servicing rights)

- Public rights (wireless spectrum rights, etc.)
- Brand equity
- Rights of publicity (social media influencer)
- Traditional knowledge

3 CHAPTER

PATENTS

Necessity is the mother of invention.
                                                   —English proverb

The inventor looks upon the world and is not contented with things as they are. He wants to improve whatever he sees, he wants to benefit the world; he is haunted by an idea. The spirit of invention possesses him, seeking materialization.
                                                   —Alexander Graham Bell

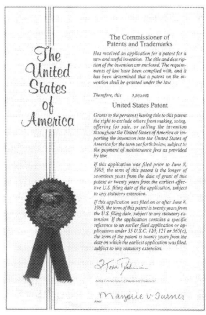

Fig. 1

Fig. 2

A patent (see Fig. 1[10] and Fig. 2[11]) for an invention is the grant of a property right to the inventor, issued by the United States Patent and Trademark Office. Generally, the term of a new patent is twenty years from the date on which the application for the patent was filed in the United States or, in special cases, from the date an earlier related application was filed, subject to the payment of maintenance fees. US patent grants are effective only within the United States, US territories, and US possessions. Under certain circumstances, patent term extensions or adjustments may be available.

The right conferred by the patent grant is, in the language of the statute and of the grant itself, *"the right to exclude others from making, using, offering for sale, or selling the invention in the United States or 'importing' the invention into the United States."* What is granted is not the right to make, use, offer for sale, sell, or import, but the right to exclude others from making, using, offering for sale, selling, or importing the invention. Once a patent is issued, the patentee must enforce the patent without aid of the USPTO.

---

[10] Fig 1 shows an older patent cover.

[11] Fig. 2 shows the newly redesigned patent cover.

There are three types of patents:

1. *Utility patents* may be granted to anyone who invents or discovers any new and useful process, machine, article of manufacture, or composition of matter, or any new and useful improvement thereof.
2. *Design patents* may be granted to anyone who invents a new, original, and ornamental design for an article of manufacture.
3. *Plant patents* may be granted to anyone who invents or discovers and asexually reproduces any distinct and new variety of plant.

Patent Laws

The patent system added the fuel of
interest to the fire of genius.
—Abraham Lincoln

The Constitution of the United States gives Congress the power to enact laws relating to patents; article 1, section 8 reads, "Congress shall have power . . . to promote the progress of science and useful arts, by securing for limited times to authors and inventors the exclusive right to their respective writings and discoveries." Under this power, Congress has, from time to time, enacted various laws relating to patents. The first patent law was enacted in 1790. The patent laws underwent a general revision, which was enacted July 19, 1952, and which came into effect January 1, 1953. It is codified in Title 35, United States Code, 35 US Code Section 100, et seq. Additionally, on November 29, 1999, Congress enacted the American Inventors Protection Act of 1999 (AIPA), which further revised the patent laws. (See Public Law 106-113, 113 Stat. 1501 [1999].)

The patent law specifies the subject matter for which a patent may be obtained and the conditions for patentability. The law establishes the United States Patent and Trademark Office to administer the law relating to the granting of patents and contains various other provisions relating to patents.

What Can Be Patented?

The patent law specifies the general field of subject matter that can be patented and the conditions under which a patent may be obtained.

In the language of the statute, any person who "invents or discovers any new and useful process, machine, manufacture, or composition of matter, or any new and useful improvement thereof, may obtain a patent," subject to the conditions and requirements of the law. The word *process* is defined by law as "a process, act, or method, and primarily includes industrial or technical processes." The term *machine* used in the statute needs no explanation. The term *manufacture* refers to articles that are made and includes all manufactured articles. The term *composition of matter* relates to chemical compositions and may include mixtures of ingredients as well as new chemical compounds. These classes of subject matter taken together include practically everything that is made by man and the processes for making the products.

Invention Must Be Useful

The patent law specifies that the subject matter must be useful. The term *useful* in this connection refers to the condition that the subject matter has a useful purpose and also includes operativeness; that is, a machine that will not operate to perform the intended purpose would not be called useful and therefore would not be granted a patent.

What Cannot Be Patented?

Interpretations of the statute by the courts have defined the limits of the field of subject matter that can be patented, thus it has been held that the laws of nature, physical phenomena, and abstract ideas are not patentable subject matter. A patent cannot be obtained upon a mere idea or suggestion. The patent is granted upon the new machine, manufacture, etc., as has been said, and not upon the idea or suggestion of the new machine.

4 CHAPTER

TRADEMARK

A trademark is a word, name, symbol, or device that is used in trade with goods to indicate the source of the goods and to distinguish them from the goods of others. A service mark is the same as a trademark except that it identifies and distinguishes the source of a service rather than a product. Trademark rights may be used to prevent others from using a confusingly similar mark, but not to prevent others from making the same goods or from selling the same goods or services under a clearly different mark.

Examples: McDonald's, Burger King, Mercedes, RadioShack, etc. A famous mark such as one of those marks listed above can be very expensive. The following, for example:

Fig. 3[12]   Fig. 4[13]

---

[12] Fig. 3 shows a trademark certificate issued by USPTO for a mark registered on the Principal Register.

[13] This symbol is used when a mark is used in commerce and has been registered

In May 2015, the acquisition of the RadioShack mark and its assets by General Wireless for US$26.2 million was finalized.

Common-Law Marks

Fig. 5[14]

Common-law mark rights are acquired simply by using the mark in the stream of commerce. The term *common-law* indicates that the trademark rights that are acquired through use are not protected by statute. Rather, common-law trademark rights stemmed from a judicially created scheme of rights under state law. Common-law trademark rights are limited to the geographic area in which the mark is used. Those rights are strengthened if the mark is federally registered. The symbol shown above may be used to indicate that the mark is a common-law mark.

Types of Marks

Word Mark (Lanham Act, Section 45)

As defined in section 45 of the Lanham Act, 15 USC §1127, a trademark is "any word, name, symbol or device or any combination thereof" that identifies and distinguishes the goods of one party from those of others and indicates the source of the goods.

Design Mark

As indicated above, a symbol can be used as a trademark. A design is also known as a stylized logo.

---

with USPTO.

[14] This symbol is used when a mark is used in commerce but has not been registered with USPTO.

Service Mark (Lanham Act, Section 3)

A service mark is a particular mark that is used to identify services rather than a product.[15]

Collective Mark

A collective mark is a trademark or service mark that identifies members of a union, cooperative, or other collective organization.

Certification Mark

A certification mark is a mark used in commerce by a person other than its owner to identify goods or services as being of a particular type. Certification marks are generally owned by trade associations or other centralized commercial groups. There are three basic categories of certification. The mark may be used to certify (1) regional or other origin, (2) material, (3) mode of manufacture, (4) quality, (5) accuracy or other characteristics of the goods or services, (6) or that the work or labor on the goods or services was performed by members of a union or other organization. (See 15 USC §1127.)

The owner of a certification mark is required to monitor and control use of the mark by others. Certification guarantees that goods or services bearing the mark possess certain characteristics. If the owner of a certification mark fails to strictly enforce the standards set for certification, the mark may be cancelled. (See 15 USC §1064.)

Family of Marks

A family of marks is defined as "a group of marks having a recognizable common characteristic, wherein the marks are composed and used in such a way that the public associates not only the individual marks, but the common characteristic of the family, with the trademark owner." (See *J & J Snack Foods Corp. v. McDonald*

---

[15] The owner of a mark is required to police a mark or otherwise waives his/her rights if the mark is infringed and no action has been taken.

Corp., 932 F.2d 1460, 1462, 18 USPQ2d 1889, 1891 [Fed. Cir. 1991].) The common element may be a term, a phrase, or a component in the nature of a prefix or suffix. The common element is called the surname of the family, even though it need not be the last part of each trademark in the family. The surname may be a syllable, word, phrase, prefix, suffix, or other shared term and need not be registered itself in order to be protected.

To be legally recognized as a family, the trademark family owner must use and advertise the trademarks in the family in concert with one another, not only individually, so that the public recognizes the family surname as identifying products or services originating with the trademark family owner. The benefit of having a family of trademarks is that other trademark owners may be prevented from using the family surname in their trademarks, even though that owner's marks may not be confusingly similar to any single trademark in the family.

The best-known and strongest trademark family perhaps is the family McDonald's Corp. has built around its *Mc* or *Mac* surname. This trademark family includes marks such as McDonald's, McDonald's hamburgers, egg McMuffin, McChicken, McDonut, chicken McNuggets, Big Mac, and others. McDonald's has created this family by advertising the marks together, promoting recognition of the *Mc* surname itself, and policing third-party use of the *Mc* surname. This trademark family is so strong that the *Mc* surname may not be used with toys, hotel services, or dental services.

The trademark owner should choose a distinctive surname, advertise, and promote the family of marks to create an association with each individual member and recognition of the surname itself as a trademark. The owner should then register the individual member trademarks.

The family of marks doctrine may be invoked by a plaintiff in inter partes proceedings relating to likelihood of confusion, but is not available to a defendant as defense against an opposer's or applicant's intervening rights.

Principal Register vs. Supplemental Register

A mark that is distinctive by virtue of either its unique characteristics or its long and exclusive use in commerce qualifies to be registered on the principal register. The mark must also be published and be successful during an opposition period.

Registration on the principal register confers certain rights, namely, (1) constructive notice to the public of the registrant's claim of ownership of the mark (see 15 USC §1072); (2) legal presumption of the registrant's ownership of the mark and the registrant's exclusive right to use the mark in commerce on or in connection with the goods/services listed in the registration (see 15 USC §§1057(b), 1115(a)); (3) a date of constructive use of the mark as of the filing date of the application (see 15 USC §1057(c)); (4) the ability to bring an action concerning the mark in federal court (see 15 USC §1121); (5) the ability to file the United States registration with the United States Customs Service to prevent importation of infringing foreign goods (see 15 USC §1124); (6) the registrant's exclusive right to use a mark in commerce or in connection with the goods or services covered by the registration can become incontestable subject to certain statutory defenses (see 15 USC §§1065, 1115(b)); and (7) the use of the United States registration as a basis to obtain registration in foreign countries.

Supplemental Register

A mark that is inherently descriptive, but that can potentially identify goods or services with a source will be listed on the supplemental register. Registration on the supplemental register is limited to marks that are in use in the US.

Trade Dress

Trade dress creates a visual impression that functions like a word trademark. There is really no difference between a word trademark in the visual trademark except that a word mark may be spoken while trade dress and color per se must be seen to make a commercial impression. That is how the US Supreme Court articulated trade dress in Two Pesos and Qualitex cases. Trade dress me include "features such as size, shape, color or color combinations, texture, graphics or even particular sales techniques." Trade dress creates a visual impression that operates like a word trademark. In Two Pesos, the US Supreme Court indicated that not only restaurant decor maybe protected as trade dress but also that restaurant—and other trade dresses—may be inherently distinctive and protectable from the moment of adoption. The colors and shapes of pill capsules have qualified as protectable to address in many cases. Further, bottle shapes have long been protected as trademarks. The curved and ribbed shape of the old Coca-Cola bottle is a registered trademark on the principal register under Reg. Nos. 696,147 and 1,057,884. The shape of a mobile gas pump, which used to have a distinctive round head, was protected as a trademark in a case where the defendant was selling non-mobile gas for more round-headed gas stations.

International Trademark

The Madrid system allows someone with a personal or business connection to one of the system's members to register and manage trademarks worldwide. It provides a convenient and cost-effective solution to file a single application and pay one set of fees to apply for protection in up to 122 countries.

5
CHAPTER

COPYRIGHT

The Congress shall have Power To promote the
Progress of Science *and useful Arts, by securing for*
limited Times to Authors and Inventors the exclusive
Right to their respective Writings and Discoveries.
—US Constitution, article 1, section 8, clause 8

copyright
all rights reserved

Fig. 6[16]

Fig. 7[17]

---

[16] Fig. 6 shows the symbol used to provide notice to the world that the work is copyrighted.

[17] Fig. 7 shows the copyright certification issued by the Library of Congress.

Copyright is a form of protection provided to the authors of "original works of authorship," including literary, dramatic, musical, artistic, and certain other intellectual works, both published and unpublished. The 1976 Copyright Act generally gives the owner of the copyright the exclusive right to reproduce the copyrighted work, to prepare derivative works, to distribute copies, to perform, or to display the copyrighted work publicly.

Copyright protection, a form of intellectual property law, keeps your original (developed independently by author) works of authorship (fixed in a tangible medium of expression) protected. Stated differently, copyright protection extends to the exclusive rights of exploitation of original literary and artistic works expressed in the form of words (text, computer software), music, images, symbols, three-dimensional objects, or combination thereof; pantomimes and choreographic works; pictorial, graphic, and sculptural works; motion pictures and other audiovisual works; sound recordings; and architectural works. Copyright protection also extends to derivative works that are works based on preexisting material, e.g., movie screenplay based on book and translations of book written in foreign language. Copyright protection applies only to the expression, not the underlying ideas, facts, systems, or methods of operation, although these forms of intellectual property are protected under a different area of the law. Different regimes treat copyright differently. For example, IP (intellectual property) regimes conferring economic rights are referred to as copyright systems, whereas IP regimes that incorporate both copyright and moral rights are referred to as authors' right. The copyright system prevails in the United States and other common-law countries, whereas authors' rights systems prevail in France and other civil-law countries.

Other rights that fall under the rubric of copyright and/or authors' right are neighboring rights and sui generis rights. In the US, sui generis protection covers the topography of semiconductor chips. That is, the law provides sui generis protection only for mask works, a stencil of the materials present on or removed from the layers of a semiconductor chip, which is used to etch the circuitry onto the chip.

International Aspects

The Berne Convention for the Protection of Literary and Artistic Works, usually known as the Berne Convention, is an international agreement governing copyright. The Berne Convention was first accepted in Berne, Switzerland, in 1886. The convention provides creators such as authors, musicians, poets, painters, etc. with the means to control how their works are used, by whom, and on what terms.

Marrakesh Treaty

The Marrakesh Treaty was adopted on June 27, 2013, in Marrakesh, Morocco, and came into force on September 30, 2016. The treaty makes the production and international transfer of specially adapted books for people with blindness or visual impairments easier. It establishes a set of limitations and exceptions to traditional copyright law.

Rights of Publicity (ROP)
Who Owns Your Image?

The rights of publicity protect an individual's persona and the profitability of that persona in commerce. This includes a person's image, voice, footprint, gestures, phrases, and more. As more people are becoming famous online in addition to influencing large audiences on Instagram and other social media platforms, one's rights of publicity are more important than ever.

The Vanna White Case

In 1991, Vanna White, the personality figure of *Wheel of Fortune*, filed suit in California's district court naming as defendants Samsung Electronics and David Deutsch Associates, which prepared the ad in 1988. In her complaint, she alleged that Samsung violated her famous personal and intellectual property rights. White said Samsung and Deustch used her likeness without her permission, violated her right to publicity under California law, and created confusion over whether or not she was endorsing its product. She accused Samsung of using a persona similar to hers. Specifically, Vanna alleged that Samsung used a persona similar to hers to sell its line of video cassette recorders through television commercials. Samsung used a robot to run a series of television commercials. The robot was dressed as a woman, turning letters like White does on *Wheel of Fortune*. Vanna White claimed that Samsung is enriching itself by profiting from her fame, fortune, and likeness without her express permission and without compensating her. White further claimed that the robot in the commercial was dressed with a gown, jewelry, and wig to strongly resemble her likeness. Samsung Electronics used the robot in the commercial along with an identical game board matching that of Vanna's *Wheel of Fortune*. Other celebrity likeness was also used in the commercial. Vanna contends, however, that she was the only one who was not compensated nor did Samsung obtain her prior permission. Samsung Electronics' ad executives referred to the commercial as the "Vanna White commercial."

Vanna White lost before the district court, which issued a summary judgment in favor of Samsung. In dismissing the complaint, the court indicated that the robot could not be mistaken for any person, including White. On June 7, 1991, Vanna appealed her case to the United States Court of Appeals for Ninth Circuit. The appeal court sustains the lower court decision stating that simply using the likeness of Vanna White was not intellectual property theft. The Ninth Circuit also rejected a request for reconsideration and hearing en banc. Vanna appealed to the Supreme Court, which rejected Samsung's argument that it has a First Amendment right to use a parody of White in its advertisement. The Supreme Court awarded more than $400,000 in damages to Vanna.

The Kim Kardashian Case

On August 1, 2019, a federal district court in California awarded to Kimberly Noel Kardashian West (Kim Kardashian) a $2.7 million default judgment in her lawsuit against Misguided Inc. Kim Kardashian is an American television personality and entrepreneur who garnered international fame for her personal life. Much of her life story was chronicled on the popular reality series *Keeping Up with the Kardashians*. In her lawsuit, she alleged that the fast fashion online retailer used her persona and likeness to sell its clothing. Said retailer repeatedly tagged her on Instagram and linked her to the retailer's e-commerce site. In her lawsuit against Misguide USA (Finance) Inc. and Misguided Limited, Kim accused the defendant of misappropriating her persona as part of its marketing and sales strategy to boost its sale of clothing online. Kim's complaint recited violations of her right of publicity, false designation of origin, and trademark infringement. Kim is also associated with Kimsaprincess Inc.

The district court granted a default judgment to the plaintiffs and awarded $2.7 million in damages to Kim. The court used a formula to come up with this amount. The court used nine unauthorized Instagram posts by Misguided at $300,000 per each post plus $59,600 in Attorney's fees, equating to the amount of approximately $2,759,600.

Instagram Influencers

An Instagram influencer is a person who has established credibility and an audience on the social media platform. The top Instagram influencers have over 1 million followers on the platform and are paid through sponsorships to promote goods and services to their audience. For people looking to establish themselves as Instagram influencers, it is critical that you protect your rights to publicity and do not allow others to take advantage of your likeness for their own personal gain.

Micro Influencers

A micro influencer is someone with between 1,000 and 1 million followers and is considered an expert in his or her respective field, such as cooking, travel, fashion, or fitness. Many are calling micro influencers the marketing force of the future due to their constant communication with their audience and close connection to their fan base. Micro influencers are quickly becoming the go-to group for companies looking to brand their products to specific niches of consumers, knowing that the micro influencer will create a personal connection between themselves and the product.

★ ★ ★

Who Owns a Celebrity's Image?

Courts have held that section 43(a) of the Lanham Act entitles celebrities to sue for trademark infringement when others use their persona without permission to suggest a false endorsement or affiliation with goods or services. This may seem quite similar to the right of publicity, but there is a salient difference. In order to prevail under the Lanham Act, a celebrity has to prove that the consuming public is likely to be confused and mistakenly believe there is an endorsement or affiliation where none exists. Under the right of publicity, the celebrity must show that the use is unauthorized, but whether there is consumer confusion is irrelevant to the outcome.

6 CHAPTER

TRADE SECRET

Do not tell secrets to those whose faith and
silence you have not already tested.
—Queen Elizabeth I

Fig. 8[18]

A trade secret protects from misappropriation a formula, process, mechanism, or compound that is used in business, known only to the owner and derives independent economic value from not being generally known. State law governs trade secrets. As the name implies, a trade secret is enforceable only as long as the underlying information is not made public.

Trade secret is the fourth type of intellectual property, in addition to patents, trademarks, and copyrights. Trade secrets consist of information and can include a formula, know-how, practice, pattern, design, instrument, compilation, program, device, method, technique, or process not generally known or reasonably ascertainable by others, which allow an entity or business to obtain economic advantage over competitors. To meet the most common definition of a trade secret, it must be used in business and give an opportunity to obtain an

---

[18] Fig. 8 conveys the confidential nature of the trade secret.

economic advantage over competitors who do not know or use it. Broadly speaking, any confidential business information that provides an enterprise a competitive edge may be considered a trade secret. There are three factors common to definitions of trade secret, namely, (1) a trade secret is not generally known to the public, (2) a trade secret confers economic advantage or benefit on its holder because the information is not publicly known, and (3) to maintain the secrecy of the trade secret, the holder exercises reasonable efforts.

The precise language by which a trade secret is defined varies by jurisdiction, as do the particular types of information that are subject to trade secret protection. However, clearly unfair practices with respect to secret information include industrial or commercial espionage, breach of contract, and breach of confidence.

How Are Trade Secrets Protected?

Contrary to patents, trade secrets are protected without registration; that is, trade secrets are protected without any procedural formalities. Consequently, a trade secret can be protected for an unlimited period of time. For these reasons, the protection of trade secrets may appear to be particularly attractive for SMEs (small-medium-enterprises). There are, however, some conditions for the information to be considered a trade secret. Compliance with such conditions may turn out to be more difficult and costly than it would appear at first glance.

On Wednesday, May 11, 2016, President Barack Obama signed into law the Defend Trade Secrets Act (DTSA) of 2016. DTSA amends chapter 90 of title 18, United States Code (commonly known as the Espionage Act of 1996), to provide federal jurisdiction for the theft of trade secrets "if the trade secret is related to a product or service used in, or intended for use in interstate or foreign commerce." Specifically, 18 USC §1836 authorizes federal civil proceedings for misappropriation of a trade secret by employees as well as foreign entities. Prior to that day, trade secret protection was a matter of state law, except in New York and Massachusetts, which adopted some version of the Uniform Trade Secrets Act (UTSA). DTSA does not preempt state law or any other provision of law. The salient provisions of the law are, among others, treble damages, immunity for confidential disclosure to the government (whistleblower) or to an attorney, notice of immunity to employees, anti-retaliation lawsuit, ex parte seizure order, injunctive relief, and exemplary damages. A defense to a claim of trade secret misappropriation includes reverse engineering, independent derivation, or any other lawful means of acquisition.

7 CHAPTER

INTERNET/WEBSITE

Fig. 9[19]

With the advent of the internet and consequently the World Wide Web (WWW), a website becomes an invaluable tool. Websites are used for a diversity of businesses, organizations, governments, schools, universities, and professionals, just to name a few. Hence a domain is necessary to launch a website. A domain can now be registered as a trademark.

Domain Names (ICANN)

Fig. 10[20]

ICANN stands for the Internet Corporation for Assigned Names and Numbers. It is an American multi-stakeholder group and nonprofit organization responsible for coordinating the maintenance and procedures of several databases related to the namespaces and numerical spaces of the internet.

---

[19] Fig. 9 is the symbol used to designate the World Wide Web (www).

[20] Fig. 10 is the separator that indicates the location (domain) of an individual.

Top Level Domain Names (gTLD) and (ccTLD)

Domain names are very popular and are now part of the bundle of rights an IP owner retains. A top-level domain name is the part of a domain that comes after the dot. For example, xxxxx.com, xxxxx.net, xxxxx.org, xxxxx.gov, xxxxx.edu, whereas a domain is the address of your website. A domain must be unique. As such, a domain can be trademarked.

The official list of all top-level domains is maintained by the Internet Assigned Numbers Authority (IANA). Having registered your domain and built a website, a web-hosting service is needed to get the website operational. A number of companies such as GoDaddy and Google provide web-hosting services. These companies use different types of hosting arrangements, such as shared hosting, dedicated server hosting, virtual private server (VPS) hosting, and cloud hosting to provide hosting services to a website owner.

Top-level domain names are divided into two types, namely, (1) generic top-level domains (gTLD) and (2) country-code top-level domains (ccTLD). Generic top-level domain names are domains that are associated with a country. Such domain names comprise. com, .net, .org, .edu, .gov. On the other hand, country-code top-level domains are associated with a country or geographical location.

Section 2
E-Commerce

Fig. 11[21]

E-commerce (or electronic commerce) is simply the buying and selling of goods (or services) over the internet. Stated differently, e-commerce is the activity of using the internet to buy or sell products

---

[21] Fig. 11 represents global transactions using the internet as transport mechanism (e-commerce).

or online services. To enable such transactions from mobile shopping to online payment encryption and beyond, internet-based technologies are utilized. For example, electronic funds transfer, electronic data interchange (EDI), and automated data collection systems are among the facilitators of e-commerce. E-commerce encompasses a wide variety of data, systems, and tools for both online buyers and sellers. E-commerce is categorized into six main types, namely, (1) B2B, which is an acronym meaning business to business; (2) B2C, which is an acronym meaning business to consumer; (3) B2A, which is an acronym meaning business to administration; (4) C2C, which is an acronym meaning consumer to consumer; (5) C2B, which is an acronym meaning consumer to business; and (6) C2A, which is an acronym meaning consumer to administration. There are three main areas of e-commerce: online retailing, electronic markets, and online auctions. E-commerce is supported by electronic businesses.

In the United States, certain electronic commerce activities are regulated by the Federal Trade Commission (FTC). These activities include the use of commercial e-mails, online advertising and consumer privacy. The Federal Trade Commission Act regulates all forms of advertising, including online advertising and states that advertising must be truthful and nondeceptive. Using its authority under section 5 of the FTC Act, which prohibits unfair or deceptive practices, the FTC has brought a number of cases to enforce the promises in corporate privacy statements, including promises about the security of consumers' personal information. As a result, any corporate privacy policy related to e-commerce activity may be subject to enforcement by the FTC.

Cloud Computing

E-commerce uses the internet to facilitate the transactions described above. The internet also made cloud computing possible. Cloud computing is the on-demand availability of computer system resources, including data storage and computing power without direct active management by the user. These computing resources reside on distant servers. The cloud refers to software and services that run on the internet instead of locally on your computing device.

Cloud computing is one idea that uses the internet as a transport system. Other ideas use the internet as a transport mechanism, for example, video conferencing, remote login, remote deposit, and the like. These are ideas that use the available technology to either bring about a new product/service or improve upon an existing product/service.

8

TRADITIONAL KNOWLEDGE

Today, intellectual property is not widely known in the world at large. Traditional knowledge (TK) as a type of intellectual property is even more obscure than its brethren, namely, patent, trademark, and copyright. This area (TK) of the law is very rich, unsettled, and rapidly evolving. Traditional knowledge is not part of most law schools' IP courses. Be that as it may, let us just say that traditional knowledge is often orally passed from one generation to the next in the form of stories, legends, folklore, rituals, songs, and certain universal laws. World Intellectual Property Organization (WIPO) defines traditional knowledge as "knowledge, know-how, skills and practices that are developed, sustained and passed on from generation to generation within a community, often forming part of its cultural or spiritual identity." An example of TK follows.

Originating in <u>Haiti</u>, *rara* is a form of festival music used for street processions, typically during <u>Easter week</u>. The music centers on a set of cylindrical bamboo trumpets called *vaksen* (which may also be made of metal pipes), but also features drums, <u>maracas</u>, <u>guiras</u> or <u>guiros</u> (a percussion instrument), and metal bells, and sometimes cylindrical metal trumpets, which are made from recycled metal, often coffee cans. The *vaksens* perform repeating patterns in hocket and often strike their instruments rhythmically with a stick while blowing into them. In the modern day, standard <u>trumpets</u> and <u>saxophones</u> may also be used. The genre though predominantly Afro-based has some <u>Taino Amerindian</u> elements to it such as the use of <u>guiros</u> and maracas.

The songs are always performed in <u>Haitian Kreyòl</u> and typically celebrate the African ancestry of the Afro-Haitian masses. *<u>Vodou</u>* is often implemented through the procession. The genre was imported to the <u>Dominican Republic</u> and is now an integral part of the Afro-Dominican music scene, where it is known colloquially as <u>Gaga</u>. In the Dominican Republic, the music is often played by the Afro-Dominican population as a cultural tribute to their African ancestors in the same manner as their counterparts in Haiti. Rara in Haiti is often used for political purposes, with candidates commissioning songs praising them and their campaigns. Rara lyrics also often address difficult issues, such as political oppression or poverty. Consequently, rara groups and other musicians have been banned from performing and even forced into exile—most notably, folk singer <u>Manno Charlemagne,</u> who later returned to Haiti and was elected mayor of <u>Port-au-Prince</u> in the 1990s.

Rara performances are often performed while marching and are often accompanied by twirlers employing metal <u>batons</u>. Performances generally begin on <u>Ash Wednesday</u> and culminate at <u>Easter weekend</u>.

"The Rara festival most likely developed during the period of colonial slavery, when enslaved Africans and Afro-Creoles in the colony of Saint-Domingue were said to parade with drums and instruments on Easter Sunday. There is also some evidence that troupes of maroons marched with drummers, horns, and singers, similarly to Rara."[11]

Traditional knowledge is not afforded the same breath of protection under United States conventional IP laws due in part to its collective ownership characteristic, but TK is nevertheless protected under a hodgepodge of conventions and sui generis measures. A recent US Supreme Court case,[22] although not directly related to TK, complicates the matter or even retards any progress in erecting a strong defense in favor of TK protection. The Supreme Court ruling favors the football team, Washington Redskins, reasoning that "names that might be considered insulting by some ethnic groups can be trademarked as a matter of First Amendment free speech." This ruling invalidates that portion of the federal law, which allows an exception to trademark rights if the names or images are disparaging, or insulting, to other persons or groups. Under this ruling, other offensive trademark owners such as Atlanta Braves, Kansas City Chiefs, and others are allowed to keep both their names and their trademark revenue. This case sends the wrong signal and hampers efforts to

---

[22] *Matal, Interim Director, United States Patent & Trademark Office v. Tam.*

enshrine into the US IP regime some well-established form of IP protection for TK. For example,[23] USPTO implemented a database[24] for the voluntary registration of indigenous insignia and symbols of state and federally recognized tribes. The database is used as a reference in examining trademark applications to refuse admittance of marks that "falsely suggest a connection with particular institutions," per 15 USC §1052(a)(2)(a).

WIPO has taken the lead and enunciated several goals to implement an international regime for the protection of TK. This effort aims at creating a structure or schema to compensate the people or cultures owning the knowledge against misappropriation by other cultures. These goals are to prevent the erosion and unauthorized exploitation of traditions, stimulate innovation and creativity based upon the traditional knowledge, protect the knowledge from misuse and distortion, and protect the knowledge insofar as the dignity and moral rights of the traditional innovators are concerned.[25] WIPO proposes two distinct avenues to protect TK. They are (1) defensive protection and (2) positive protection. "The defensive protection refers to a set of strategies to ensure that third parties do not gain illegitimate or unfounded IP rights over TK. These measures include the amendment of WIPO-administered patent systems (the International Patent Classification system and the Patent Cooperation Treaty Minimum Documentation). Some countries and communities are also developing TK databases that may be used as evidence of prior art to defeat a claim to a patent on such TK. WIPO has developed a toolkit to provide practical assistance to TK holders on documenting TK." WIPO is exploring two aspects of positive protection of TK by IP rights. One aspect would be directed toward preventing unauthorized TK use, whereas the other aspect would be directed toward active TK exploitation by the originating community itself.

Currently, three broad approaches to protect traditional knowledge have been developed. The first emphasizes protecting traditional knowledge as a form of cultural heritage. The second looks at

---

[23] Michigan State International Law Review, vol. 21:3, p.769.

[24] Native American Tribal Insignia Database USPTO (June 27, 2011), www. uspto.gov/trademarks/law/tribal/index.jsp.

[25] WIPO Report on Fact-finding Missions on Intellectual Property and Traditional Knowledge (1998–1999), p. 70.

protection of traditional knowledge as a collective human right. The third, taken by the World Trade Organization (WTO) and WIPO, investigates the use of existing or novel sui generis measures to protect traditional knowledge.

In its efforts to implement an international regime for the protection of TK, the United Nations via different committees organized several conferences to further its policies and goals. On September 29 to October 17, 2003, at its thirty-second session, UNESCO (United Nations Educational Scientific and Cultural Organization) met in Paris, France, to discuss the issues related to TK protection. The meeting was held under the banner of "Convention for the Safeguarding of the Intangible Cultural Heritage." The report[26] of the meeting cited and made reference to the Universal Declaration of Human Rights of 1948.

During its thirty-third session on October 3 to 21, 2005, UNESCO met again, this time under the banner "Convention on the Protection and Promotion of the Diversity of Cultural Expression" to continue the discussion on the protection of TK. The report[27] of the meeting is also provided for further reading if so desired.

The third approach involves novel sui generis measures to protect traditional knowledge. In the United States, on July 12, 1999, the USPTO held a public hearing on official insignia of Native American tribes. As discussed above, these efforts have to be revisited.

---

[26] See appendix D.

[27] See appendix E.

9 CHAPTER

WHERE DO I SECURE MY INTELLECTUAL PROPERTY?

The question of where or what agency to contact to secure a particular type of intellectual property depends on the character of that property. For example, if you have created some kind of gadget that functions a certain way, you will need to secure a patent. In this case, you will have to file for a patent at the USPTO to secure protection in the United States. If protection is desired elsewhere in the world such as China, Europe, and Africa, then you can request that your US patent application be recognized in these jurisdictions.

If you also want to give a catchy name to this new gadget, giving a brand name, you will want to file for a trademark, which is also administered by the USPTO for the United States. International protection can be acquired as discussed later below in the trademark section. However, if your idea is to write a book or a movie, you will have to file for a copyright, which is administered by the Library of Congress. The sections following will introduce you to different offices and their function as part of the whole intellectual property system.

★ ★ ★

USPTO
The United States Patent and Trademark Office

Congress established the United States Patent and Trademark Office to issue patents on behalf of the government. The Patent Office as a distinct bureau dates from the year 1802 when a separate official in the Department of State, who became known as Superintendent of Patents, was placed in charge of patents. The revision of the patent laws enacted in 1836 reorganized the Patent Office and designated the official in charge as Commissioner of Patents. The Patent Office remained in the Department of State until 1849 when it was transferred to the Department of Interior. In 1925, it was transferred to the Department of Commerce where it is today. The name of the Patent Office was changed to the Patent and Trademark Office in 1975 and changed to the United States Patent and Trademark Office in 2000.

The USPTO administers the patent laws as they relate to the granting of patents for inventions and performs other duties relating to patents. Applications for patents are examined to determine if the applicants are entitled to patents under the law, and patents are granted when applicants are so entitled. The USPTO publishes issued patents and most patent applications eighteen months from the earliest effective application filing date and makes various other publications concerning patents.

The USPTO also records assignments of patents, maintains a search room for the use of the public to examine issued patents and records, and supplies copies of records and other papers, and the like. Similar functions are performed with respect to the registration of trademarks. The USPTO has no jurisdiction over questions of infringement and the enforcement of patents.

The head of the office is the Under Secretary of Commerce for Intellectual Property and Director of the United States Patent and Trademark Office (Director). The director's staff includes the Deputy Under Secretary of Commerce and Deputy Director of the USPTO, the Commissioner for Patents, the Commissioner for Trademarks, and other officials. As head of the office, the director superintends or performs all duties respecting the granting and issuing of patents and the registration of trademarks; exercises general supervision over the entire work of the USPTO; prescribes the rules, subject to the approval of the Secretary of Commerce, for the conduct of proceedings in the USPTO and for recognition of attorneys and agents; decides various questions brought before the office by petition as prescribed by the rules; and performs other duties necessary and required for the administration of the United States Patent and Trademark Office.

The work of examining applications for patents is divided among a number of examining technology centers (TCs), each TC having jurisdiction over certain assigned fields of technology. Each TC is headed by group directors and staffed by examiners and support staff. The examiners review applications for patents and determine whether patents can be granted. An appeal can be taken to the Patent Trial and Appeal Board from their decisions refusing to grant a patent, and a review by the director of the USPTO may be had on other matters by petition. In addition to the examining TCs, other offices perform various services, such as receiving and distributing mail, receiving new applications, handling sales of printed copies of patents, making copies of records, inspecting drawings, and recording assignments.

Functions of the United States Patent and Trademark Office

The United States Patent and Trademark Office is an agency of the US Department of Commerce. The role of the USPTO is to grant patents for the protection of inventions and to register trademarks. It serves the interests of inventors and businesses with respect to their inventions and corporate products and service identifications. It also advises and assists the president of the United States, the secretary of commerce, the bureaus and offices of the Department of Commerce, and other agencies of the government in matters involving all domestic and global aspects of intellectual property. Through the preservation, classification, and dissemination of patent information, the Office promotes the industrial and technological progress of the nation and strengthens the economy.

In discharging its patent related duties, the USPTO examines applications and grants patents on inventions when applicants are entitled to them; it publishes and disseminates patent information, records assignments of patents, maintains search files of US and foreign patents, and maintains a search room for public use in examining issued patents and records. The Office supplies copies of patents and official records to the public. It provides training to practitioners as to requirements of the patent statutes and regulations, and it publishes the Manual of Patent Examining Procedure to elucidate these. Similar functions are performed relating to trademarks. By protecting intellectual endeavors and encouraging technological progress, the USPTO seeks to preserve the United States' technological edge, which is key to our current and future competitiveness. The USPTO also disseminates patent and trademark information that promotes an understanding of intellectual property protection and facilitates the development and sharing of new technologies worldwide.

Overview of the World Patent System

Since the rights granted by a US patent extend only throughout the territory of the United States and have no effect in a foreign country, an inventor who wishes patent protection in other countries must apply for a patent in each of the other countries or in regional patent offices. Almost every country has its own patent law, and a person desiring a patent in a particular country must make an application for a patent in that country in accordance with the requirements of that country.

The laws of many countries differ in various respects from the patent law of the United States. In most foreign countries, publication of the invention before the date of the application will bar the right to a patent. Most foreign countries require that the patented invention must be manufactured in that country after a certain period, usually three years. If there is no manufacture within this period, the patent may be void in some countries; although in most countries, the patent may be subject to the grant of compulsory licenses to any person who may apply for a license.

There is a treaty relating to patents adhered to by 176 countries (at the time of this printing), including the United States, and is known as the Paris Convention for the Protection of Industrial Property. It provides that each country guarantees to the citizens of the other countries the same rights in patent and trademark matters that it gives to its own citizens. The treaty also provides for the right of priority in the case of patents, trademarks, and industrial designs (design patents). This right means that on the basis of a regular first application filed in one of the member countries, the applicant may, within a certain period of time, apply for protection in all the other member countries. These later applications will then be regarded as if they had been filed on the same day as the first application. Thus, these later applicants will have priority over applications for the same invention that may have been filed during the same period of time by other persons. Moreover, these later applications, being based on the first application, will not be invalidated by any acts accomplished in the interval, such as, for example, publication or exploitation of the invention, the sale of copies of the design, or use of the trademark. The period of time mentioned above, within which the subsequent applications may be filed in the other countries, is twelve months in the case of first applications for patent and six months in the case of industrial designs and trademarks.

Another treaty, known as the Patent Cooperation Treaty, was negotiated at a diplomatic conference in Washington, DC, in June 1970. The treaty came into force on January 24, 1978, and is presently (as of 2014) adhered to by over 148 countries, including the United States. The treaty facilitates the filing of applications for patents on the same invention in member countries by providing, among other things, for centralized filing procedures and a standardized application format.

The timely filing of an international application affords applicants an international filing date in each country, which is designated in the international application and provides (1) a search of the invention and (2) a later time period within which the national applications for patent must be filed. A number of patent attorneys specialize in obtaining patents in foreign countries.

Under US law, it is necessary, in the case of inventions made in the United States, to obtain a license from the director of the USPTO before applying for a patent in a foreign country. Such a license is required if the foreign application is to be filed before an application is filed in the United States or before the expiration of six months from the filing of an application in the United States unless a filing receipt with a license grant is issued earlier. The filing of an application for a US patent constitutes the request for a license and the granting or denial of such request is indicated in the filing receipt mailed to each applicant. After six months from the US filing, a license is not required unless the invention has been ordered to be kept secret. If the invention has been ordered to be kept secret, the consent to the filing abroad must be obtained from the director of the USPTO during the period the order of secrecy is in effect.

★ ★ ★

World Intellectual Property Organization (WIPO)

WIPO is the global forum for intellectual property (IP) services, policy, information, and cooperation. WIPO is a self-funding agency of the United Nations, with 192 member states.

Its mission is to lead the development of a balanced and effective international IP system that enables innovation and creativity for the benefit of all. Its mandate, governing bodies, and procedures are set out in the WIPO Convention, which established WIPO in 1967.

★ ★ ★

Where Should You File for Your IP Protection

This is a complex question. It depends on what the owner wants to accomplish and budget as outlined in the IP strategy document if one exists. Generally, you would want to protect your right in markets where your invention or idea is likely to be used and be subject to theft. You should also consider protecting in countries with strong intellectual property regimes and strong enforcement. Patent protection is local. This means that you must have a patent in each country that you would like to have protection. However, for Europe, there is a way to file one application that would be recognized by all member countries under the Patent Cooperation Treaty (PCT). However, if you need protection in the member countries, you must convert your application to a localized application. Similarly, there are other regional agencies that provide the same scope of protection, for example, if protection is sought in Africa.

For trademark, you should consider registering your mark in any country or jurisdiction where you offer your products or services under that mark, as well as in those countries/jurisdictions where you intend to use the mark for your products or services in the future. Use of a mark is not a prerequisite for filing an application in most countries and jurisdictions; however, some do have use requirements.

Similarly, for copyright, you must apply in each country. In practice, you would apply in the countries that you think your work would most likely be infringed and where you believe if infringement happens that you can find legal remedies. See appendix C for a list of websites of different country's intellectual property offices.

The following are examples:

African Intellectual Property Organization OAPI (Organisation Africaine de la Propriété Intellectuelle; African Intellectual Property Organization) was formed by members of certain French-speaking African nations. The organization enables applicants to file a single application for protection of a trademark in designated countries that are contracting parties to the Bangui Agreement, which created OAPI. The contracting parties are Benin, Burkina Faso, Cameroon, Central African Republic, Chad, Comoros, Republic of the Congo, Côte d'Ivoire (Ivory Coast), Gabon, Guinea, Guinea Bissau, Equatorial Guinea, Mali, Mauritania, Niger, Senegal, and Togo.

The European Patent Office/Patent Cooperation Treaty (PCT) is an international treaty with more than 150 contracting states. The PCT makes it possible to seek patent protection for an invention simultaneously in a large number of countries by filing a single international patent application instead of filing several separate national or regional patent applications. The granting of patents remains under the control of the national or regional patent offices in what is called the national phase.

10 CHAPTER

DO I NEED AN ATTORNEY?

There are three (3) types of people: those who see; those who see when they are shown; and those who do not see.
—Leonardo da Vinci

We hope the previous chapters of this book have provided some basic information to help you create a plan to start taking advantage of your ideas knowing that you have to take steps to protect them. After reading this book, it is our hope that you will stop renting your ideas to others and give them away for free or just let them die in the idea graveyard. But we don't pretend that you will find all the steps easy to protect your rights.

With everything in life, you can probably do it yourself with some research and perseverance. However, while you know you could probably learn how to make the clothes that you are wearing right now, you probably did not. You had preferred to buy it from a professional tailor or seamstress. The reason is simple: it will save you time, and it will probably be done with a higher quality.

The laws are written for anyone to apply for their own rights in the United States. In some countries, you may be required to hire a lawyer. But even in the US, many choose to use a lawyer to secure their rights.

It is advisable to always consult with a professional in the field. Those professionals are best placed to guide you in the process. There are many pitfalls that can be avoided by using a professional that may not be intuitive to a layperson. The attorney will charge a fee, and sometimes the fees may seem prohibitive. But the attorney can save you money in the long run and also save you time. This may allow you to introduce your product quicker to the market and avoid pitfalls that may result in less rights or no rights at all.

For patents, the prosecution process can be very complex. It requires the filer to follow many rules and to respond to office correspondence in a specific amount of time. If a response time is missed, there could be extra fees or even abandonment of your invention. The filer would have to respond to office action and draft arguments to the examiner to reconsider your cases. The file would have to learn how to draft effective claims and do amendments to them as part of response. In short, while it is possible and that the law in the US does not preclude an inventor from filing *pro se* (by yourself), tread carefully if you decide to take on the task on your own.

Patent attorneys are members of a state bar and also the patent bar, which is administered by the USPTO. They often have a technical background, and they often practice in the patent field within their field of expertise—so a person with a background in electrical engineering would work in the invention of electrical engineering. Some patent attorneys do not have a technical background (this is rare), they tend to just do litigation work.

Patent agents are not attorneys, but they are registered agents in front of the USPTO to represent an inventor. Patent agents can help with the prosecution of a case in front of the USPTO but usually are not versed on other aspects of intellectual property. In short, both a patent attorney and patent agent can guide you through the process of getting a patent. In the IP world, a patent is often referred to as *hard IP*, whereas trademark and copyright are referred to as *soft IP*.

Trademark attorneys are intellectual property attorneys. They don't necessarily need a technical degree. They are all attorneys and members of at least one state bar. They have experience prosecuting trademarks before the US Patent and Trademark Office. Because trademark registration is a legal proceeding with strict procedures and deadlines, a lawyer who is familiar with the process can handle registration more efficiently than you can on your own. Again, the law does not preclude you from filing for your own trademark, but it may become challenging if you are not sure of what you are doing or if you don't have the time to learn the process.

Just like trademark attorneys, copyright attorneys are IP attorneys, and they don't need a technical degree. They are all attorneys and members of at least one state bar. The process of registering a copyright work does not entail subtle issues as trademark; therefore, a copyright owner may not need an attorney to register the work. However, when the copyright is infringed, then the help of an attorney is sine qua non because copyright law is very complex. With everything else that deals with legal matters, when you are not sure or even if you are sure, consult with an attorney to make sure that you are taking the right steps.

In selecting any lawyers to help you to procure your intellectual property rights, you must do your due diligence. In the resource section, you will find a link to the USPTO. The office publishes a list of registered agents who are allowed to practice in front of the office. Also, you can start your search in the bar association of each state to find a licensed attorney in your state. We are sure such resources are also available in the country where you live if you reside outside the United States. Intellectual property is a very specialized field of law, so make sure that the lawyer you select practices IP and, if you plan to apply for a patent, that the lawyer is registered with the US Patent office.

11 CHAPTER

VALUING YOUR INTELLECTUAL PROPERTY

Expect the best. Prepare for the worst.
Capitalize on what comes.

—Zig Ziglar

What is the value of a particular IP asset? The answer to this question is not easily discernible. There are many methods of evaluation techniques, but none of them offer a result that can be adopted as the definitive value. In fact, these valuation techniques can produce different values for the same technology. Further, each of these techniques suffer from inherent limitations by failing to account for certain economic factors in the different models. In short, there is no panacea; one must do one's due diligence. The reader will appreciate however that although these methods have limitations, used together, they provide a very powerful and useful decision-making tool.

Valuation Methods

In general, there are three basic approaches of valuation: the cost approach, the market approach, and the income approach.

The *cost method* seeks to measure the future benefits of ownership by quantifying the amount of money that would be required to replace the future service capacity of the subject property.[28]

---

[28] See Gordon Smith, International Workshop on Management and Commercialization of Inventions and Technology, WIPO (April 2002), p. 3. The market approach is the most direct and the most easily understood appraisal techniques.

The *market approach* values an asset based upon comparable transactions between unrelated parties. "It measures the present value of future benefits by obtaining a consensus of what others in the marketplace have judged it to be."[29]

The most frequently used in IP valuation is the *income approach*.[30] The income approach focuses on a consideration of the income-producing capacity of property.

The mathematics needed to carry out the different approaches are discussed in Smith and Parr.[31]

Other Valuation Developed For Use in Intellectual Property Transactions

In addition to these basic valuation methods, there are seven commonly used methods developed for use with intellectual property. These methods are as follow:

A. *25 percent rule.* This method calculates a royalty as 25 percent to 33 ⅓ percent of the gross profit, before taxes, from the enterprise operations in which the licensed intellectual property is used. The advantage of this method is that it is easy to apply, but the disadvantage is that it is very inaccurate—it does not take into account the environment. For example, two patents can generate the same gross profit, but one requires more cost to generate profit. One may require substantial advertising cost. It also fails to consider risk and fair rates on investment.

B. *Industry norms.* This method focuses on the rates that others are charging for intellectual property licenses within the same industry. The disadvantages of this method: reliance on the ability of others to correctly consider all the factors affecting royalties; mistakes in the initial setting are passed along.

---

[29] Id., p. 3. The market approach is the most direct and the most easily understood appraisal techniques.

[30] Harvard Business School, *Intellectual Asset Valuation*, Dec. 2, 2000.

[31] Gordon V. Smith and Russell L. Parr, *Valuation of Intellectual Property and Intangible Assets*, 3rd ed. (New York: John Wiley & Sons Inc., 1999).

C. *Ranking method.* This method compares the intellectual property asset to be valued to comparable intellectual property assets on a subjective or objective scale.

D. *Surrogate method.* This was developed to value patents. The three most common types of surrogate measures are the number of patents issued to a company, payment of patent maintenance fees, and prior art citations.

E. *Disaggregation method.* There are two basic types of disaggregation methods: value and income disaggression. *Value disaggregation* seeks to apportion some fraction of total value to intellectual property assets by setting the value of intangible assets equal to the value of a firm. *Income disaggregation* seeks to apportion some fraction of total earning of a firm, based upon various factors.

F. *Monte Carlo method.* This method is primarily used as a refinement of the income method. Whereas the income method assigns a single value to the variables used in calculating the net present value (NPV) of an asset, the Monte Carlo method assigns a range of value to the variables.[32] There

---

[32] See Hagelin, Supra, 1133, 1134–1135. "The 25 Percent Rule is the most simple . . . licensor should receive 25 percent of licensee's gross profit from the licensed technology. The industry standard is widely used . . . it attempts to value an IP asset by reference to royalty rates in similar past transaction . . . information about royalty rate is available from several different sources such as . . . Security Exchange Commission, court decisions [www.royaltysource. com] . . . The ranking method compares the intellectual property asset to be valued to comparable intellectual property assets on a subjective or objective scale . . . Surrogate measures have been developed to value patents . . . the three most common types of surrogate measures are the number of patent issued to a company, payment of patent maintenance fees, and prior art citations . . . There are two basic types of disaggregation methods—value and income disaggregation. Value disaggregation seeks to apportion some fraction of total value to intellectual property assets by setting the value of intangible assets equal to the value of a firm . . . minus the firm's monetary assets . . . and tangible assets . . . Income disaggregation seeks to apportion some fraction of total earning of a firm, based upon various factors . . . The Monte Carlo method . . . is primarily used as a refinement of the income method . . . Whereas the income method assigns a single value to the variables used in calculating the net present value (NPV) of an asset, the Monte Carlo method assigns a range of value to the variables . . . The option methods . . . are based on . . . the Black-Scholes formula. Under the Black Scholes formula, the

are also a number of other new and less known methods, for example, the *competitive advantage valuation* (CAV) and the *econometric patent valuation methods* and others

Reasons for Valuation

There are many reasons why intellectual property assets have to be evaluated. Often IP is valuated for the purpose of support of a transaction, for example, a transfer of an IP asset. However, the valuation of an IP asset may be carried out for reasons other than the actual selling or buying an IP asset. Some other common reasons include, but are not limited to, corporate valuation for shareholders, corporate mergers and acquisitions, management, initial public offering (IPO), financial reporting, licensing IP asset, IP donation, and litigation. The literature suggests that different IP valuation methods are more suitable for one situation than another.

---

essence of a stock option's value lies in the right to wait and see what happens to a stock's price and to exercise or not to exercise . . . the adaptation of [] this valuation to intellectual property is based on the same "wait and see" value."

12 CHAPTER

MONETIZING YOUR
INTELLECTUAL PROPERTY

In managing a company/your IP assets, it is often necessary to "engage in technology triage: exploiting high-priority patents [and other IPRs] and abandoning others." The abandoned technology is placed in a category often referred to as orphan technology. According to BTG international technology transfer consultancy, 35 percent of the typical US company's patented technology falls in this category.[33] Further, "a private study noted that 67 percent of U.S. companies own technology assets they fail to exploit. The value of these wasted assets in the U.S. accounts for more than $115 billion."[34] For this reason, today more than ever, IP managers and other IP practitioners need to investigate and apply different methods to extract the value of the company's IP assets. Below are a few ways that a manager should be considering in developing a method to optimize the value of a company's assets.

Must Have a Strategy

At the outset, it should be emphasized that any intellectual property management effort should start with a strategy. The IP strategy that one chooses must be synchronized with the overall business strategy. A typical intellectual property management model

---

[33] David C. Drews, *The Benefits of Patent Donation* (IPMetrics, Feb. 22, 2001). See also www.corporateintelligence.com.

[34] John Wahl, "Mining Intellectual Property in Tech Field Could Be Golden," *Denver Business Journal* (2003).

would include an inventory phase, assessment phase, strategy phase, and deployment phase. Once an IP management strategy is in place, the organization is ready to start harvesting the reward of having and developing intellectual property. And because there is no one perfect method available, the implemented IP strategy must be measured (reevaluated) to evaluate the effectiveness of the plan.

Different Options for IP Management

Generally, companies have five options for managing their technology. They can use, sell, license, donate, or abandon their IP assets. "A company with a strong value extraction strategy [should] employ all these approaches to ensure . . . maximum returns on every dollar invested in research and development (R&D)."[35] In each other these options, IP valuation may be different. A brief description of each option (with emphasis on licensing and donation) follows.

Licensing

You can make money for an IP that you own. For example, if you have an idea to create a machine, you can patent it as an invention. If you are granted the patent by the USPTO, then you can make the product or simply license it to another company to make the product and pay you a royalty. The bundle of rights referred to above includes licensing and assignment. Licensing in many cases is the preferred form of exploitation of a particular IP asset. Generally, there are three types of licenses, namely, (1) express license, (2) implied license, and (3) compulsory license. Most IP can be licensed. Some examples include music licensing, dramatic performance licensing, software licensing, etc. Detailed discussion about these licenses are beyond the scope of this book.

In a license, the technology owner and the licensee divides the future economic benefit according to the terms of a license. The rights are divided, and the relative risks to be borne by the licensor and licensee determine how the economic benefit will be shared. The licensee typically pays for these rights in the form of royalty.

[35] Myron A. Marcinkowski, Donating Intellectual Assets (2000)

Companies also often engage in cross-licensing by exchanging access to specified technologies within their respective portfolios. Cross-licensing often results when companies are trying to fend off infringement suits.

In the context of licensing, although different methods of valuation are used in practice, the income approach is the preferred method. This method estimates the economic benefit of the licensee, considers the parties' relative risks, considers the costs of exploitation and who will bear them, and calculates the present value of the benefit to which the licensor is entitled. Each of the methods are being used in the industry as methods for arriving at a particular royalty. The reader should note each of these methods have their own shortcomings.

Determining the financial worth of your IP asset, as the reader may already appreciate, is not a cake walk. Generally, IP valuation is a work for economists or other trained in this field. But with the advent of computer-aided tools, there may be help for you in the near future. These software tools are becoming available to support an IP manager in the licensing or other processes. Watch for artificial intelligence to solve the problem.

Anyways, we do wish that you do not get hanged up in this idea of what your IP worth yet; we simply wanted to introduce you to the topic and to plant in your mind, "Someday, after I have created my intellectual property asset portfolio, there are ways to value such assets and many ways to extract the value of such assets."

Assignment

Generally, an IP owner may assign all her/his rights in the protected subject matter. An assignment is also referred to as a transfer in which the owner relinquishes *vitam eternam*, all rights inherent and appurtenant to the owner of the assigned IP. Such transfer includes the right to make use of the assigned IP absent a license back from the assignee. Once the transfer is finalized, the assignee assumes all rights, including the right to license the IP without, any hindrance. A true assignment is found when the right holder gives all rights and does not even retain the right to terminate the agreement. Otherwise, such assignment will be deemed a license rather than assignment.

Patent as an Asset

As indicated above, IP is the commodity and currency of the information age, i.e., the twenty-first century. For example, in 2016, intellectual property asset transactions accounted for more than 20 percent of world trade, or approximately US$740 billion. Compared to this amount today, just in the United States, 52 percent of all US merchandise exports is IP based or approximately $6.6 trillion (38.2 percent of GDP). Experts in the field who are cognizant of the data observed that in the past three decades or so, "the United States and developed world economies have experienced an economic inversion transforming from manufacturing into tangible asset-lite, innovation-based economies. This transformation is one of the most underexploited developments in contemporary economics, finance and investing." As a result, the banking industry added a new investment portfolio serving parties interested in IP-driven deal structures. Patents can be bought and sold at auctions just like any other property. More and more in bankruptcy situations, patents are listed as properties, which carry a value just like any other property.

13

INTELLECTUAL PROPERTY
AND THE COURTS

"In today's knowledge-driven economy, IP rights have become valuable business assets. Most successful companies in recent years have relied heavily on their creative and innovative capacity as their main source of competitiveness. Such inventiveness, know-how and creativity are captured and transformed into exclusive business assets through the acquisition of IP rights. This is why IP protection offers an important tool for businesses to enhance competitiveness and strengthen the position of their products or services in the marketplace."[36]

IP is not self-enforced. As a result, when and if misappropriation or infringement of IP occurs, one may have recourse to the US court system. As another branch of government, the US legal system is very complex. This section only provides a very limited aspect of the action an owner of intellectual property may contemplate. In no way can this section be considered legal advice. Consultation with an IP attorney is required if legal advice is needed.

The court system is a very important component in the IP system. It is the place where disputes are resolved in a civil manner. Intellectual property is also policed by their owners. This means that you, the property owner, must take action to protect your IP rights. However, the US government also has a few enforcing agencies (customs, FBI, to combat IP theft in general; see the resource page for more agencies involved in IPR enforcement).

In order to actually have a property, one must be able to enforce their rights regarding that property. It is common knowledge that our

---

[36] WIPO - IP Management & Commercialization of new Products, p. 3, ¶9.

real estate property is protected by laws and violating them may result in legal repercussions. For example, if a person trespasses on someone else's property, they may be charged for trespassing and taken to court for that infraction. If a person takes your property or damages your real or tangible property, you can likewise take them to court. This is not different for intellectual property. Intellectual property enforcement relies on both the civil and criminal courts, state and federal. Further, intellectual property is subject to the general antitrust principles that apply to the conduct involving any other form of property. "That is not say that intellectual property is in all respects the same as any other form of property. Intellectual property has important characteristics, such as ease of misappropriation that distinguish it from many other forms of property."[37] "The intellectual property laws and the antitrust laws share the common purpose of promoting innovation and enhancing consumer welfare. The intellectual property laws provide incentives for innovation and its dissemination and commercialization by establishing enforceable property rights for the creators of new and useful products, more efficient processes, and original works of expression. In the absence of intellectual property rights, imitators could more rapidly exploit the efforts of innovators and investors without providing compensation. Rapid imitation would reduce the commercial value of innovation and erode incentives to invest, ultimately to the detriment of consumers. The antitrust laws promote innovation and consumer welfare by prohibiting certain actions that may harm competition with respect to either existing or new ways of serving consumers."[38]

When a person or company takes or uses your intellectual property, e.g., patents, trademarks, copyrighted works, etc., without the owner's permission (without a license), this is an infringement to your rights. Most unlawful taken in IP is handled under civil laws in the United States; therefore, it is often not referred to IP theft, although IP theft can be the appropriate term in some cases, especially when it involves trade secrets.

IP theft is a very serious problem. In fact, the total theft of US trade secrets accounts for anywhere from $180 billion to $540 billion per year, according to the Commission on the Theft of American Intellectual Property.

---

[37] Antitrust Guidelines for the Licensing of Intellectual Property issued by the US Dept. of Justice and the Federal Trade Commission, Jan. 12, 2017, p. 3.

[38] Antitrust Guidelines for the Licensing of Intellectual Property issued by the US Dept. of Justice and the Federal Trade Commission, Jan. 12, 2017, p. 2.

Intellectual property disputes are resolved in both state and federal courts. Exactly in what situation that one system is used versus another is not the subject of this book. However, the lion share of lawsuits regarding IP is brought in the federal court system. Further, the federal system has very specialized courts to adjudicate over appeals over IP (Patent Trial Appeal Board, Trademark Trial Appeal Board, district courts, Court of Appeal of the Federal Circuit, and Supreme Court).

This section was not meant to be comprehensive on how the courts are involved in protecting intellectual property rights, but it should make you aware that the courts play a pivotal role in securing the right once they are acquired. Some recent judgments and amounts are shown in the table to give you an idea of the magnitude of money that courts (judges) or juries have awarded to IP owners.

Table 1

Company	IP Type	Controversy	Award
Erickson v. Kast[39]	Copyright	Use of photograph	$450,000
Apple v. Samsung	Patent	Design of phone	$539,000,000
Tiffany v. Costco	Trademark	Use of trademark	$14,000,000
BMG v. Cox[40]	Copyright	Music piracy	$1 billion
USAA v. Wells Fargo	Patent	Mobile check deposit	$200,000,000
Sloan Kettering Institute v. Kite Pharma Inc.	Patent	CAR T-cell therapy	$1.2 billion
Wal-Mart v. Variety	Trademark	"The Backyard"	$95,000,000
Kim Kardashian v. Misguided Inc.	ROP/ Trademark	Use of likeness	$2,759,600

These infringement awards should make it clear for you that intellectual property generates a lot of money, and when your intellectual property rights are infringed (taken without your permission), the infringer can pay a significant amount of money to the property owner. The courts will make sure that the owner's right is protected and just compensation is awarded.

[39] *Erickson Prods. Inc. v. Kast*, 2019 BL 134449, 9th Cir., No. 15-16801, 4/16/19.

[40] *BMG Rights Mgmt. (US) LLC v. Cox Commc'n. Inc.*, Nos. 16-1972, 17-135 (4th Cir., Feb. 1, 2018).

14 CHAPTER

INVENTIONS THAT HAVE
SHAPED THE 2010 DECADE

Obviously, many inventions contributed to our lives in the last decade. In a way, all the inventions have somehow shaped the landscape. Many technological advances have happened during the last decade. We discuss some of the inventions not in an exhaustive way, but just to highlight those game-changers.

We saw the continuous releases of the handheld devices, like the iPhone, Samsung and Google phone, etc. These devices changed the way we communicate (like FaceTime), the way we bank, and how we interact with the internet.

We also saw the larger device known as tablets (*iPad tablet computer*) granted various patents, e.g., US Patent No. 9,621,611, USD 687,030. This device has changed how we read a book, read our newspapers in the morning, watch movies, etc. With these devices, we can interface and control many items in our homes, like turning on and off the lights in the house, setting the thermostat, answering the door with "Ring," or the like. One device, which facilitated such functions is the Nest thermostat, which was granted US Patent No. 9,605, 858 B2 and US D 503,631.

Smart watches changed the way we exercise and how we monitor our health—a watch is not just a device to keep time, but it also has additional functions, such as pulse monitor, tracking distance, path traveled, etc. *Smart watches* (wearable device) various patents (see e.g., US D 879,628).

We basically have an app for everything we want to do. We could call for a ride (taxi) using our devices from Uber or lift. We could even hail a *self-driving car* (various patents, see e.g., US Patent Nos. 10/557,940; 10/591,600). We have an app to fetch our food at our favorite resto, and it is at our door in a minute. We also have an app to give us access to our movies. Of course, TV has also changed; we all watch our shows on demand and from sources other than regular channels. We seek content at very high resolution on our 4K TVs where the picture is reproduced in near perfection.

These self-driving cars are made possible by *artificial intelligence*,[41] which is the brain. In the future, our car will pick us up on command, and it will go park itself until it is needed again. It will be smart. It will drive itself to the garage when service is due. AI also made possible *virtual assistants* (various patents, see e.g., US Patent No. 8,107,401) in the likes of Alexa, Siri, Google, Watson, and many more.

We also saw the advent of teleconferencing that has allowed for people to collaborate at far distances as if they worked in the same office. We observed more and more face-to-face meetings are replaced by video conferencing. As we write this book, we are under a stay-at-home order due to the coronavirus commonly referred to as COVID-19. This technology is being used by all sectors of the society, from work, school, government, and family to stay connected. Millions of Americans and others all around the world are teleworking during confinement. Technology is the glue that connects us all.

Another technology that influenced the last decade are *drones* (US Patent No. 9,488,978). They have allowed us to see the world from a bird's-eye view. We can now travel over the neighborhood and survey our roof by taking pictures from a perspective of the sky. Drones are also poised to become more invasive in our lives as research and development continue to fine-tune it as a delivery tool. Soon, your package will not be delivered in the traditional way via a personal courier, but a drone safely dropping you package in your property or softly landing to place your property in short proximity to your front door.

The *3D bioprinting* (various patents, see e.g., US Patent Nos. 8,691,974, 9,183,764, 10/392,595, 10/463,871) allows for literally printing an object from your screen to a printer.

GPS, while not an invention of the past decade, really became commonplace in all new cars as a utility that we no longer can live

---

[41] Artificial intelligence is a subgroup of machine learning, robotics, neural network, and computer vision.

without. Now, when we can drive to any location without knowing how to get there, all we need is the address, and this app will find the best route to get there.

We also saw technology bring back to life dead celebrities via a technology called hologram (see the *dead celebrity holograms*).[42]

The innovations were not just in electronics but also in biotech. *CRISPR* (clustered regularly interspaced short palindromic repeats; various patents, see e.g., WO 2016110512 A1) is a family of DNA (deoxyribonucleic acid) sequences found in the genomes of prokaryotic organisms such as bacteria and archaea. These sequences are derived from DNA fragments of bacteriophages that had previously infected the prokaryote. They are used to detect and destroy DNA from similar bacteriophages during subsequent infections.[43]

All these inventions started as an idea. They were developed to machines, software, and processes and brought to the marketplace. Different trademarks are used to identify the products. They were made by someone just like you. You have the capacity to take your ideas to the next level and bring us new technology. All you need to do is take action and make sure that you heed advice from this book to seek intellectual property rights. Just remember, "the journey of a thousand miles begins with the first step."

---

[42] Invented by Englishmen Henry Dircks and John Henry Pepper.

[43] Wikipedia.

15 CHAPTER

INVENTIONS THAT WILL SHAPE THE NEXT 20 YEARS

Technology will undoubtedly dominate our future. The advent of computers have revolutionized the way we do everything, from typewriting and accounting to keeping files. The personal computer provided us with one tool on our desk that helped us become more efficient. Networking allowed us to connect to one another without going from office to office, while the internet connected us to the world.

The mobile phone allowed us to take and have our conversation wherever there is a signal available. The first generation (1G) made it possible to transmit analog signal voice. The second generation (2G) introduced us to digital voice. The third generation (3G) brought us mobile data and texting. The fourth generation (4G) and 4G LTE ushered the mobile broadband, allowing you to stream, watch videos, and listen to music; and it allowed you to use your mobile device, like your iPhone, iPad, and the like to be used like your desktop personal computer. 4G LTE increased the speed that data can be transmitted by ten times the speed available in 3G. Today, you can do all your transactions from your mobile device, from playing games to watching your favorite shows to shopping for your weekly groceries. This would be unimaginable just about fifteen years ago.

5G will revolutionize yet again the way we perceive technology and how we use it. 5G is the next generation of wireless networks that will altogether change the way we live our lives, interact with one another, travel, and do work. It will be a remarkable paradigm shift. 5G is not just going to increase the speed at which we can download a movie, but it is true that the speed will be about a warping hundred times the 4G LTE. Wow! This means you will be able to download your favorite movies in a second of a time.

More importantly, 5G will allow for technology that does not exist today to come to fruition. You will be able to send a hologram of yourself as opposed to FaceTime. 5G will allow the world to be fully connected through the Internet of Things (IOT). All your home appliances will be connected to the internet, and your home will be totally automated and interactable from anywhere around the world.

5G will make the way you travel very much different than the way we travel today. I joke with my kids that they may be the last generation to have a driving license. The next generation will know autonomous car and drone delivery of food and items they purchase online. Robots will do the chore at home and do many tasks that are today done by humans.

Autonomous cars or driverless cars will become more and more commonplace. These cars will be smart and will coordinate with other cars to avoid collisions, thus no more accidents. I think you will be glad to drop your car insurance or have to pay a reduced monthly premium. The cars will be run by artificial intelligence (AI).

★ ★ ★

Artificial Intelligence

Artificial intelligence (AI) makes it possible for machines to learn from experience, adjust to new inputs, and perform humanlike tasks. Examples of AI today are Siri, Alexa, etc. These software answer questions, perform a search for you on Google, and read you the findings. They can also help you lock and unlock doors, turn on and off your lights, and find and play your favorite song—all with a simple voice command. Now and in the future, AI will enable smart robots. These very smart robots will be police officers, factory workers, and maybe even inventors.

Artificial intelligence (AI), a branch of computer science, is a constellation of technologies grouping generally two main technical fields, namely, symbolic learning (SL) and machine learning (ML). Advances in hardware enable AI implementation. Such advances will likely facilitate innovation and thereby expand the field of AI.

AI attempts to mimic human intelligence. For example, a human navigates the outside world moving from place to place and all the while making decisions by using sensory data like sounds recorded by the ears, images and symbols captured by the eyes, temperature sensed by the skin, and smell perceived by the nose. Using these data, the brain computes a reality within the temporal and spatial dimensions.

Conventionally, symbolic learning, which falls under image processing, comprises two main branches namely, robotics and computer vision.

Machine learning (ML) is also divided into two main branches to wit: statistical learning and deep learning. Generally, machine learning is used for classification (e.g., identifying patterns with large volumes of business data) or prediction (smart algorithm). In pattern identification, if the machine is left to figure out the pattern, some in the industry refer to it as unsupervised learning. On the other hand, if a trained algorithm with an answer is used, then it's referred to as supervised learning.

Statistical learning is further divided into speech recognition and natural language processing (NLP). Deep learning involves neural networks. Neural network as a field of AI has evolved into convolution neural networks (CNN), recurrent neural networks.

By way of background, the earliest neural net, the perceptron, was developed in the 1950s. It was considered the first step toward human-level machine intelligence. However, a 1969 book by MIT's Marvin Minsky and Seymour Papert entitled *Perceptrons* proved mathematically that such networks could only perform the most basic functions.

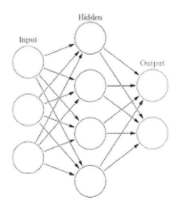

A simple neural network diagram

It was not until 1986 that Hinton showed that back propagation could train a deep neural network, and the advancement of computer technology renewed interest in neural networks. Even though AI made great strides, much work remains to be done. "After all, today's neural networks are based on decades-old architecture and a fairly simplistic notion of how the human brain works, "says Jacob Vogelstein, a neural network scientist. Efforts are under way in different universities and research centers to map the brain of rats in order to obtain some answers to the many questions regarding how the human brain works. For example, the real brain is full of feedback: for every bundle of nerve fibers conveying signals from one region to the next, there is an equal or greater number of fibers coming back the other way, says M. Mitchell Waldrop, a neurologist working on the mapping project.

The increased interest in AI results in tremendous growth of patent protection for AI in the US. However, as may be expected, in the US, the law about AI is unsettled. Two recent Court of Appeals for the Federal Circuit (CAFC) decisions, i.e., *Berkheimer v. HP* and *Aatrix Software v. Green Shades Software*, have not provided any bright line rule concerning adjudication of AI. In fact, the indication is that there is an increased likelihood that decision by a finder of fact will be required in any issues involving AI. In Europe, AI and machine learning are largely unpatentable and are per se "of an abstract mathematical nature." The European Patent Office will look closely at whether claimed subject matter has a technical character as a whole. As a result, expressions such as "neural network" and "reasoning machine" usually refer to abstract models and are therefore unpatentable.

Quantum Computing

Quantum computing is the next wave in computer technology. A quantum computer uses photons that exhibit quantum effects as the underlying transport mechanism, whereas a digital (classical) computer uses electrons and/or the absence of electrons as the underlying transport mechanism. A classical computer has a memory made up of bits (0, 1), where each bit represents a one or zero. A quantum computer maintains a sequence of qubits. A qubit (see e.g., US Pat. No. 8,461,862) is the quantum equivalent of a bit. However, unlike a bit, a qubit can be in multiple states simultaneously. For example, a qubit could be a 0, 1, or both at once. That permits faster calculations for some problems and also poses certain challenges, because keeping qubits stable has proved difficult. In comparison, when the same phenomenon occurs in digital computer, such as when the output of a flip-flop oscillates between 0 and 1, the flip-flop is said to be in metastable state, yielding to a certain delay in ascertaining the specific state (either 0 or 1) of the flip-flop. Thus, this unwanted result leads to the quest for improving the response time of the basic devices of a digital computer. In its October 11, 2013, volume 13, issue 638, the weekly magazine *The Week* reported a breakthrough in material engineering that may lead to means for hauling data in the next generation of quantum computers. Physicists from MIT and Harvard have engineered a new form of matter that behaves "just like a lightsaber," the report stated. "For the first time, scientists have managed to clump together photons—massless particles of light that don't normally interact with one another—to form a molecule. When two lasers are aimed at one another, their beams typically pass through one another. But the photonic molecules created here push against and deflect each other," said Harvard physicist Mikhail Lukin.

As an emerging field, quantum technology could transform information processing and confer big economic and national-security advantages to countries that dominate it. As quantum computing is implemented, thereby displacing classical computers, this will constitute a paradigm shift requiring a buffer, allowing the two systems to coexist until classical computers leave the scene. There will be a transition period reminiscent of when desktop computers replaced mainframe computers (using punch cards and running COBOL, FORTRAN). Desktop computers were much smaller and faster than mainframes. It was a significant change. However, this time, it will be even more dramatic. It's back to the drawing board. Quantum computing ushers in a new era in the information age unlike anything before it. As mainframe computers faded away, some companies like DEC (Digital Equipment Corporation) and CDC (Control Data Corporation) also went away, but others like IBM (International Business Machine) survived. New actors like Compaq, Commodore International, TI (Texas Instrument), HP (Hewlett Packard), Sun Microsystems (Solaris, Java, etc.), Microsoft (DOS, Windows), Apple (Macintosh), and others appeared on the scene. So, too, this time, this paradigm shift will be a crisis for some and an opportunity for others. There will be winners and losers. For example, companies like TI (Texas Instruments) lost the desktop battle.

Space.com ran an article entitled "Quantum Supremacy Is Here." Study coauthor Brooks Foxen, a graduate student researcher in physics at Google AI Quantum in Mountain View and the University of California, Santa Barbara, states, "A computation that would take 10,000 years on a classical supercomputer took 200 seconds on our quantum computer" In sum, based on this study the quantum computer is 1.5 trillion (1.5×10^{12}) times faster than the classical computer. With such computing power, the digital revolution with associated hardware architecture, software, network topology, and IT (information technology) will be transformed.

Teleportation

Quantum technology is poised to impact teleportation in a big way. Teleportation is the hypothetical transfer of matter or energy from one point to another without traversing the physical space between the two points. For example, using quantum entanglement, a trip from New York City to Paris, France, would be done in a fraction of the time it would take an airplane.

Nanotechnology

Nanotechnology—the world is shrinking, and in the future, we will all be touched by this technology. Your handheld device will get smaller and will be able to perform more complex tasks. For example, your phone will soon have a projector included in it that will be able to project 3D imaging. You will hear more about this product called graphene, which is only one atom tall. It is 150 times stronger than steel, almost completely transparent, and 150 times more conductive than silicon. Using this material will again revolutionize and catapult technology as never seen before. For example, it will increase battery life in your devices, computers will get to one thousand times faster than today's machines, and your device's screen will be pliable and unbreakable.

In the future, you may have robots—well, nanobots—go through your bloodstream to clear, for example, a blood-clot. What are nanobots? you ask.

"Not to be confused with these fictional nanorobots, for medical nanotechnology researchers, a nanorobot, or nanobot, is a popular term for molecules with a unique property that enables them to be programmed to carry out a specific task. These nanobots are a reality and are being actively researched and developed."[44]

For example, nanobots and cancer—"The *nanobots* traveled through the bloodstream, targeted the blood vessels around *cancerous tumors*, and released blood clotting drugs to cut off the blood supply to the tumours. According to the study, the treatment was successful in shrinking the tumours and inhibiting their spread."[45]

This may sound very futuristic, but in reality it is here.

Cryptocurrency

Already today, it is rare that you see a person paying with real money or paper cash. Today, people are using more credit cards or debit cards. In a sense, money is now digital, but this is not what we mean by cryptocurrency. Money transactions today are centralized via a bank/credit card company like Visa or MasterCard. The bank is the entity that provides the trust between the buyer and seller over the internet; without the bank in between, the seller would not send the product to the buyer until the seller received the money, and the buyer would argue that the seller sends the product before the seller pays. In the past, this was solved by cash on delivery (COD) by the postman—well, that would be a backward evolution.

Well, how else could two people who don't know each other or don't trust each other do business over the internet if the middle man (i.e., the bank) is unwanted? This problem is solved by this new technology called blockchain.

"The most basic definition of blockchain is a shared, digitized ledger that cannot be changed once a transaction has been recorded and verified. All parties to the transaction, as well as a significant number of 3rd parties maintain a copy of the ledger (i.e. the

---

[44] https://www.nanowerk.com/what-are-nanobots.php.

[45] https://www.futuresplatform.com/blog/can-we-use-nanobots-cure-cancer.

blockchain), which means it would be practically impossible to amend every copy of the ledger globally to fake a transaction."[46]

This is the technology that Bitcoin, Ethereum, Libra, and many other cryptocurrencies are based on. Cryptocurrencies are a digital form of money that runs on a totally new monetary system, one that is not regulated by any centralized authority or tracked by a formal institution. There are many types of cryptocurrency with various functions. Regardless of each function, each digital currency is supported by a decentralized peer-to-peer network called the blockchain. Blockchain technology ensures that all cryptocurrencies are kept track of, regardless if they are being held in a digital wallet or being used in trading. In the future, we all will have a digital wallet to keep our cryptocurrencies, and we will make all our financial transactions using cryptocurrencies, no doubt about it.

Blockchain also will permeate our lives in other ways, like smart contract and supply chain, and will change the way we cast our votes. In order words, there will be plenty of space to apply new ideas and contribute to the future of technology and humanity. Your ideas could be the one to move these technologies forward, and this is why it is important for you to take action and not let your idea perish in the mind.

Technology and the Law

New technology will certainly change laws. When inventions start creating their own inventions—for example, an AI software composes a piece of music or paints a painting or even creates a new robot—who will be the composer, artist, or inventor? Who will be the owners of such works? Currently, the laws would attribute the rights to the person(s) who have created the work. Now, is the owner created by an AI unit or robot the property of the owner of the AI software or robot? The law is not clear on such matters today. This new phenomenon will probably require that IP laws be updated in many ways.

---

[46] https://cointelegraph.com/tags/blockchain.

Future Technology and Humanity

The future is full of technologies that will continue to change the way humans live their lives.

Technology is a tool and, like any tools, can be used for good—to advance humanity to new heights; however, technology can also be used in a way that hurts humanity. It is important to always strike the right balance. As a tool, it should serve the greater good, and technology must be available to all. If it is not, future technologies will widen the gap between the haves and the have-nots, and the social imbalances will worsen. Technology should serve humans to become more human—more time to think, travel, and be social. Technology should connect us in a way that is just not possible today. It should help us appreciate that we have one world and that we are one people. Our lives are intertwined, and to truly be human means that we see one another and that we all have equal opportunity to contribute to the journey. Together, humans can use technology to "boldly go where no man has gone before."

You and Future Technology

Remember that your ideas are not small, and they also have a place in the future. You must find ways to bring your ideas to the world using the technology of the day, and if the technology does not exist, create it. It may not be your culture to create or to follow your ideas to make it a product. Maybe you have tried before and it did not work out as expected. Perhaps, you have ideas but are not sure that it will work out, afraid of what people will say about your idea. Know that it is possible. If you never turn your ideas to reality, technology may not grow to its fullest.

We hope that this book has motivated you to take action toward making your idea a reality. As Steve jobs eloquently said, "When you grow up you tend to get told that the world is the way it is and your life is just to live your life inside the world. Try not to bash into the walls too much. Try to have a nice family life, have fun, save a little money. That's a very limited life. Life can be much broader once you discover one simple fact: Everything around you that you call life was made up by people that were no smarter than you. And you can change it, you can influence it . . . Once you learn that, you'll never be the same again."

16 CHAPTER

CONCLUSION

In reading this book about intellectual property and how it can be used to protect your ideas if they are developed in such a way to be protected under one of the schemes of IP laws, we hope that this book enticed you to learn more about the subject and to always take action to develop your idea. In today's information age, the products of the mind are becoming more and more valuable. You can own your ideas and even make money out of them. Your idea may be the next big thing, so you owe it to the world to bring it to reality. Take action now, contact an attorney, or research the US Patent Office for more information on how you can protect your invention and register your trademark. Contact the Library of Congress to register your literary and artistic work, register your website, create a contact list, or start a podcast. Whatever your idea is, it will not be more if you don't take any actions.

What Is Your Big Idea Now?

If you can believe it, you can achieve it.
—Unknown

Go take action now and make it a reality. Ideas come to you for a reason. It is the universe talking to you. It may be your "why" that you are here alive in the first place—that you were born to bring this new thing, this new book, this new movie to the world. You are entrusted with this idea for all of us. If you don't take action, you may be depriving the whole humanity of this idea. You must believe that you can make it happen. The world is counting on you to take action. We wish you much success as you bring your idea to the world. Don't forget to write to us and let us know how successful you become after reading this book.

Ideas + Action = Success
Success may be defined by money
Therefore
Ideas + Action = Money

APPENDIX A

THE NEED FOR SIGNAL CLAIMS
Albert DeCady and Emmanuel Coffy*

ABSTRACT

In recent years, the scope of 35 USC 101 has substantially narrowed. In 2005, the United States Patent and Trademark Office (USPTO) issued interim Guideline disqualifying the so-called "signal claims" as patent eligible subject matter. The CAFC (Court of Appeals for the Federal Circuit) in its decision in In re Nuijten sustained the position of the USPTO essentially excluding these types of claims as patent eligible subject matter. The Decision in Nuijten is one such decision curtailing the scope of 35 USC 101. This paper specifically analyzes the need for signal claims. This paper also looks at other recent Court decisions, which further reduce the scope of patent eligible subject matter. This paper calls for a return to the liberal view expressed in Diamond v. Chakrabarty and for Congress to intervene by codifying Chakrabarty.

The Need for Signal Claims
Albert DeCady[1]and Emmanuel Coffy[2], [3]

SUMMARY

In view of the recent decision of *In Re Petrus A.C.M. Nuijten*,[4] signal claims are deemed directed to non-statutory subject matter and thus, not eligible for patent protection. This decision, however, appears to be inconsistent with precedents and the intent of Congress.

A signal claim recites a signal[5] either explicitly or impliedly. A propagated signal claim is directed to transient manufactured phenomenon, such as an electrical, optical or acoustical signal. The first signal claim was patented by Morse[6] in 1853. In 1972,[7] some 130 years later, the Supreme Court adjudicated that signal claims were no longer patentable subject matter.

However, eight (8) years later in 1980,[8] in *Diamond v. Chakrabarty*, the Supreme Court announced that "Congress plainly contemplated that patent law would be given wide scope . . . [embracing] the notion that the scope of patentable subject matter includes 'anything under the sun that is made by man.'" Under this doctrine, a signal continued to be patentable subject matter until 2005 when the United States Patent and Trademark Office (USPTO) issued an Interim Guidelines disqualifying "claims that recite nothing but the physical characteristics of a form of energy, such as a frequency, voltage, or the strength of a magnetic field and as such are nonstatutory natural phenomena." The USPTO decision led to the rejection of Nuijten's Claims 14 and 22-24 in part under 35 U.S.C. §101. The Board of Appeal and Interferences affirmed the Examiner's decision and Nuijten appealed to the Court of Appeals for the Federal Circuit (CAFC). The CAFC affirmed the Board's decision and Nuijten appealed to the Supreme Court.

Now, the Supreme Court is poised to review the case. If the Supreme Court affirms the lower court, it would sound the death knell for signal claims, leaving Congress to act if signal claims were to see the light of day under the current patent regime. We believe it would be proper and indeed prophylactic for Congress to formulate the legislative policies aimed at providing some equilibrium in this area of the law. One way to achieve this objective would be to codify *Chakrabarty*.

I. INTRODUCTION

In Re Petrus A.C.M. Nuijten was decided by the United States Court of Appeals for the Federal Circuit (CAFC) on September 20, 2007. This decision, however, appears to be inconsistent with precedent and the intent of Congress when it carved the language of 35 U.S.C.

§101.[9] The issue before the Court in this case was whether a transitory signal is covered by any statutory category under 35 USC §101. In *Nuijten*, the majority upheld the position of the USPTO that a signal claim does not fit in any of the four statutory categories (process, machine, manufacture, or composition of matter) as set forth in section 101. "The majority [based] its decision on the Century Dictionary definition of manufacture quoted by the Supreme Court in *American Fruit Growers, Inc. v. Brogdex Co.*[10] and in *Diamond v. Chakrabarty:*[11] 'the production of articles for use from raw or prepared materials by giving to these materials new forms, qualities, properties, or combinations, whether hand labor or machinery.'" [12] The majority concluded that this definition limits the term "manufacture" to non-transitory, tangible things. We believe this decision is contrary to precedent and detrimental to the progress of science, especially in this contemporary world in which we live where every process, method or software program is sold and transmitted via signals which are modulated and used as a container or storage device to deliver such method or program. This article proposes that the CAFC's textual interpretation of the law is rather narrow. It does not embrace the spirit of the law, the intent of Congress and appears to be anachronistic.

In *Chakrabarty*, the Court announced that by choosing expansive term such as "manufacture" "Congress plainly contemplated that patent law would be given wide scope."[13] "Accordingly, Chakrabarty embraces the notion that the scope of patentable subject matter includes 'anything under the sun that is made by man.'"[14] As indicated by the dissent in *Nuijten*, "the majority does not follow the guidance the Supreme Court provided in Chakrabarty as to how to interpret §101."[15]

This article analyzes the complex issue of signal claims in the Internet age when technology is changing[16] at a very fast pace. Recognizing a paradigm shift in the onward march of science, the article proposes a balanced approach to the issue at hand. The article postulates the duality that a signal is a natural phenomenon whereas a signal *with a specific content* is an article of manufacture as well. As a natural phenomenon, a signal should not be eligible for patent; however, as an article of manufacture, a signal modulated with specific content should be eligible for patent. This principle is analogous to the "no preemption" doctrine and the notion that "claim must be considered as a whole" enunciated by the United States Patent and Trademark Office.[17], [18]

II. WHAT IS A SIGNAL CLAIM?

As the name implies, a signal claim recites a signal[19] either explicitly or impliedly. A propagated signal claim such as an electrical, optical or acoustical signal is directed to transient manufactured phenomenon. For example, the signal claim of Nuijten reads as follows:

> A signal with embedded supplemental data, the signal being encoded in accordance with a given encoding process and selected samples of the signal representing the supplemental data, and at least one of the samples preceding the selected samples is different from the sample corresponding to the given encoding process. [Claim 14].

Propagated signal claims offer unique advantages in obtaining patent protection for data communications inventions and software inventions where the software is transported over and/or interacts with a propagation medium. Just as with article of manufacture claims, propagated signal claims increase the breadth of patent coverage.[20] It provides patent owners protection against infringers who produce and transport software on propagation media.[21]

III. HISTORY OF SIGNAL CLAIMS

The issue of whether a signal claim is eligible for patent is not new. A signal claim was found to be patentable subject matter in 1854 when the Supreme Court upheld the patentability of one of Samuel Morse's patents in what would today be termed a "signal claim."[22] This decision marks the genesis of a very long period in the history of signal claims as patentable subject matter until the abrupt and apocalyptic decision handed down by the CAFC last year.[23] Signal claims enjoyed the status of patentable subject matter for over a century. However, signal claims were no longer patentable when the Supreme Court decided *Gottschalk v. Benson,* some 130 years following Morse.[24] A breakthrough for signal claims was announced in *Chakrabarty,* when the Supreme Court enunciated the principle "anything under the sun that is made by man." Then, in *Diamond v. Diehr*,[25] the Supreme Court indicated that a process may be patentable if it contains a law of nature or a mathematical algorithm, thus satisfying 35 U.S.C. §101 and is patentable subject matter. Next, the Federal Circuit in *In re Alappat*[26] decided that new and useful computer software is patentable subject matter if it has a practical application that produces concrete, useful and tangible results. That decision was affirmed in *In re Lowry*.[27] With *In re Beauregard*,[28] computer programs embodied in a tangible medium such as floppy diskettes were eligible to be patented. Suddenly, in 2005, the USPTO issued an Interim Guidelines disqualifying "claims that recite nothing but the physical characteristics of a form of energy, such as a frequency, voltage, or the strength of a magnetic field, define energy or magnetism, per se, and as such are nonstatutory natural phenomena." It continued: "Moreover, it does not appear that a claim reciting a signal encoded with functional descriptive material falls within any of the categories of patentable subject matter set forth in Sec. 101."[29]

On September 20, 2007, the CAFC issued two decisions pertaining to 35 U.S.C. § 101:[30] *In re Stephen W. Comisky*[31] and *In re Nuijten*. Both decisions curtailed the scope of what is considered patentable subject matter under §101. *Comisky* "limits the arguable scope of the *State Street Bank* decision by requiring a pure mental process be connected to a machine (e.g., a computer) in order for a claim to recite subject matter that can be patentable, under the so-called section 101."[32] In *Nuijten*, the Federal Circuit examined the patentability of signal claims. "The issue before the court was whether or not a signal is patentable subject matter. Petrus A.C.M. Nuijten appeals the decision of the Board of Patent Appeals and Interferences ("Board") of the United States Patent and Trademark Office ("USPTO"), which rejected claims 14, 22, 23, and 24 in his patent application Serial No. 09/211,928 as unpatentable subject matter outside the scope of 35 U.S.C. § 101."[33] The Board affirmed the Examiner's rejection that the "signal" claims in Nuijten's application are not directed to statutory subject matter.[34] Subsequently, the CAFC affirmed the Board's decision. This case is now pending before the Supreme Court on petition for writ of certiorari.

IV. WHY SIGNAL CLAIMS ARE NEEDED?

Simply stated, signal claims are needed to encourage innovation in the age of molecular nanotechnology (MNT), thus, promoting the progress of science and useful arts, which is the primary purpose of the U.S. patent laws.[35] With the advent of many new technologies such as the Internet, Personal Data Assistant (PDA), cell phone and the like, many transactions are occurring with a signal as both a transport mechanism (carrier) and content (modulated). One such transaction, for example, is the downloading of software. Before the commercialization of the Internet, a software company would sell software via some form of diskette, which was later replaced by newer technology such as laser disc and DVD.[36] However, today, most of software sales occur online. In some instances, the process allows an end user to interact with software residing on a distant server. The transaction is carried out via a series of signals communicated between the end user and the server to carry out a specific function.

Currently, while the legal position continues to suggest that a process/method/program ("article") stored on a computer readable medium, such as a disc, is statutory subject matter, after the decision in *Nuijten,* this same patented process/method/program, which recites an embedded signal, is non-statutory subject matter. Therefore, under current patent law, a patent owner is left with little protection from infringement occurring by modulating and/or transmitting a patented process/method/program.

If signals are not patentable, it becomes difficult for patent owner to fully protect its inventions in today's environment. Let's review this scenario to analyze the problem. A user (user 1) buys a copy of patented software from a company and loads the same unto a server, which user 1 owns. Since user 1 can legally load the software by purchasing a license,[37] user 1 does not infringe by having the software stored on computer readable media (in this case on the hard-drive of the server). User 1 also does not infringe from carrying the process of such a program because he has a license. User 1 decides to make this patented article available for download from his server to all who want to have a copy from the Internet.[38], [39] Under the Court's ruling, since an article modulated on a carrier is not manufactured and thus non-statutory and ineligible for patent, user 1 is not infringing the article, which is now made available for download or transmission.

Another user (user 2) who wants to have access to the article without having to pay for a license, downloads, stores and makes use of the same without ever paying for the invention made and owned by another. User 2 infringes the invention for having said article stored on a computer readable medium (user 2's computer hard drive or disc) and is presumably making use of the same, thus infringing said article. User 2 is subject to direct infringement[40] suit under patent law, but not the person (user 1) who makes the patented invention available for download.[41], [42] As articulated above, user 1 may be a contributory infringer,[43] but cannot be held liable for direct infringement.

To avoid this problem, there is a need to provide protection at the distribution point (here user 1). It would forbid the person (user 1) making the article available for download; thus making such a person a direct infringer of the invention. Such violation would subject the infringer to suit under the patent laws. Without this protection, patent owners are left without a direct way to protect their property. In search to find ways to protect patent owners, practitioners are obliged to find creative ways of claiming signals. This added complexity would almost certainly increase the cost of drafting applications directed to these types of inventions.

Second, signal claims could potentially reduce the number of claims in a patent application by eliminating the filing of separate sets of transmitter and receiver claims, since a manufacturer of a transmitter ora receiver that uses the infringing signal will directly infringe a propagated signal claim.[44]

Third, literal infringement[45] of a signal claim could be ascertained if a competitor illegally transmits the signal via the Internet to an end user.[46]

V. MAN-MADE SIGNALS QUALIFY AS "MANUFACTURE"

Computers permeate the ubiquitous Internet. The flow of signal constitutes the "life blood" of a computer. Computers communicate via signals. A computer, to be operational, communicates with its peripheral (support) devices through a local bus via signals. Likewise, a computer communicates with the outside world via signals. A signal is a practical application that produces a tangible result. The result of the application of such signals is readily measurable and because it enables the function of the systems in which it is implemented—enables useful results in the operation of the computer systems. A signal, whether transmitted via a wire or wireless technology, can be a unique signal specifically designed to convey specific information or data.[47] The type of signals referred to herein is the product or output of a microprocessor, peripheral device or the like. These signals do not occur in nature. They are the product of a device such as a microprocessor. If they do not occur in nature and they are not a process, machine, manufacture or composition of matter,[48] it then begs to ask what are they?

It is clear a signal is not composition of matter or a machine.[49] A signal is not a process either since a process is a series or sequence of steps.[50] The last category is a manufacture or articles of manufacture. Does a signal fall under the rubric of manufacture? To answer this question, we need to ask: how is manufacture defined? We turn to a modern dictionary for the definition of this term.

Due to the progress of science and useful arts, we come to understand many phenomena that for the longest evade our understanding, albeit, there are plenty more we may not understand. For example, it is not too long ago when Stephen Hawkins[51] spoke of a blackhole. We come to understand that the world is made up of 90% of dark matter. Although its presence is felt, it cannot be seen. Accordingly, as industry retools with new technology, so too our lexicon expands: new terms are added and old ones take on new meaning. For sure, manufacture is no longer what it used to be. The term has evolved. We need to use the modern definition of manufacture, which is more in harmony with present day science and reflects the latest techniques in manufacturing. Manufacture refers to tangible articles or commodities[52] and tangible means "able to be perceived as materially existent."[53] If a signal exists in the real world and has tangible causes and effects (may be sensed or perceived), it is therefore, tangible."[54] A signal such as the one claimed by Nuijten is not an abstract idea, neither is it a law of nature nor a natural phenomenon. The dissent in *Nuijten* remarked that in *Chakrabarty*, the Court held that a genetically-engineered bacterium was patentable because it was "non naturally occurring manufacture or composition of matter—a product of human ingenuity having a distinctive name, character [and] use."[55] Likewise, Nuijten's watermarking[56] signal has a distinctive name; it has a specific character and use. If Nuijten's watermarking signal is tangible and is the output of a device; thus, it is the product of manufacture stemming from a process. It follows that a signal is an article of manufacture notwithstanding its transitory nature.

To be fair, many believe that signal claims serve no purpose because "Signals only become interesting or valuable when they make machines do things."[57] We beg to differ with this view. As proposed above, there exists a hole in the protection for a patented process, method or program if such patented method, process, or program can be distributed freely without infraction of the patent laws.

It is also worth noting the concerns on "innocent infringers"[58] such as Internet Service Providers (ISPs) and telecommunication companies. There is a potential claim for contributory infringement[59] or vicarious infringement.[60] Furthermore, the inherently transitory nature of signals and the potential for this characteristic of signals to result in ill-defined or overly broad claims requires strict adherence to the requirements of 35 U.S.C. §112.[61] We propose a safe harbor similar to those established in the Digital Millennium Copyright Act (DMCA) for ISP and other innocent infringers providing vital services, which made the fabric of the World Wide Web (WWW).[62]

We conclude this section by quoting Thomas Jefferson: "Ingenuity should receive a liberal encouragement."[63] Signal claims should be patentable because they are a means of producing a beneficial result or effect.[64] Communication of signal is and will continue to play a significant role in the information age. This area of technology is also evolving as new demand for better technique of communication drives the need for innovation. To exclude this technology outright from patentable subject matter is bad policy and will not serve to promote this technology, which was the purpose of the patent law in its inception.

VI. IS THERE A NEED TO AMEND 35 USC §101?

Congress last modified §35 U.S. C. 101 in 1952.[65] This amended version of the statute states:

> Whoever invents or discovers any new and useful process, machine, manufacture, or composition of matter, or any new and useful improvement thereof,

may obtain a patent therefore, subject to the conditions and requirements of this title.

Compared with the previous versions of the statute, "not much change [was made] in the way of the categories of patentable subject matter."[66] The categories were slightly changed from "art, machine, manufacture, or composition of matter" to "process, machine, manufacture, or composition of matter." The 1952 Act also created separate section to deal with whether a particular invention sought to be patented is novel and non-obvious.[67]

In the history of the statute, it is never made clear whether the enumerated categories, i.e. process, machine, manufacture, or composition of matter, "are merely examples of patentable subject matter, or whether these categories are limitations on patentable subject matter."[68] As a result, since the beginning of this republic, the courts have struggled with patentable subject matter. The pendulum has gone full swing many times over. At times, the courts have broadened the view of patentable subject matter and other times the courts have curtailed the scope of patentable subject matter.[69] This issue of proper interpretation of this section continues to plague the courts today and the United States Patent Office and its Examiners who have to decide daily on this issue.

This article proposes that the liberal view announced by the Court in *Chakrabarty* is the correct view of interpreting this section of the law. In *Chakrabarty*, while the Court embraced the notion of "anything made by man," the Court also cautioned that section 101 had limits. "The laws of nature, physical phenomena, and abstract ideas have been held not patentable."[70] This is a good result. Under this regime, all invention made by man is eligible for patent under 35 U.S.C. §101. This is not to insinuate, however, that every invention made by man is worthy of a patent. The U.S. Patent Office and its highly professional and knowledgeable staff is well capable of sorting out inventions that are not worthy of a patent under other sections of the statutes. [71] Subject matter eligibility under 101 is only one test. There are other hurdles to overcome before a patent is issued. Recently, the Court issued a seminal decision dealing with the proper guideline for obviousness.[72] Following these guidelines, inventions that are not worthy of a patent can be dealt with by applying prior art and other rationale provided by the Court.

Only allowable processes are granted patents.[73] A patentable process embedded on a carrier wave does not result in an act of nature. This process should be protected from infringement by protecting the very act of transmitting such patented process to avoid mass distribution to potential infringers. As it was mentioned above, it is too costly to enforce patent by suing individual users, it is impractical, and it does not make good business sense. Therefore, there is a need to provide protection for these types of claims.

Nuijten filed a writ of certiorari to the Supreme Court. Respondent's reply brief is due by August 13, 2008. The decision of the Supreme Court may very well determine the fate of signal claim. Let us examine some possible scenarios.

The Supreme Court may remand the case. In *Chakrabarty*, the Court once held that Congress chose the expansive language of 35 U.S.C. §101 so as to include "anything under the sun made that is made by man."[74] The Court stated:

> In choosing such expansive terms as "manufacture" and "composition of matter," modified by the comprehensive "any," Congress plainly contemplated that the patent laws would be given wide scope. The relevant legislative history also supports a broad construction. The Patent Act of 1793, authored by Thomas Jefferson, defined statutory subject matter as "any new and useful art, machine, manufacture, or composition of matter or any new or useful improvement [thereof]." Act of Feb. 21, 1793, ch. 11, Sec. 1, 1 Stat. 318. The Act embodied Jefferson's philosophy that "ingenuity should receive a liberal encouragement." V Writings of Thomas Jefferson, at 75-76. See Graham v. John Deere Co., 383 U.S. 1, 7-10; 148 USPQ 459, 462-464) (1966).

Subsequently, the Federal Circuit did acknowledge this principle. The Court held, "The use of the expansive term 'any' in §101 represents Congress's intent not to place any restrictions on the subject matter for which a patent may be obtained beyond those specifically recited in §101 and the other parts of Title 35." The USPTO followed and adapted the doctrine by concluding: "Thus, it is improper to read into §101 limitations as to the subject matter that may be patented where the legislative history does not indicate that Congress clearly intended such limitations."[75]

If the Supreme Court affirms the CAFC, the game is over. It would be the death knell of signal claims. Then it would be left to Congress to consider amending 35 U.S.C §101.

VII. TIME FOR CONGRESS TO ACT

The language of 35 USC § 101 "Whoever invents or discovers any new and useful <u>process, machine</u>, <u>manufacture, or composition of matter</u>, or any new and useful improvement thereof, may obtain a patent thereof" has remained unchanged, except for the substitution of "process" for "art," since the 1793 Patent Act. Congress in its wisdom has appropriately chosen expansive language to define the four categories of statutory inventions to protect the full scope of technological ingenuity. It was always the intent of Congress that these terms would be given their broadest interpretation. In *Chakrabarty*, the Court observed, "Congress plainly contemplated that the patent laws would be given wide scope."[76] "*Chakrabarty* embraces the notion that the scope of patentable subject matter includes 'anything under the sun that is made by man.'"[77] Under this notion, invention that is nothing more that a mere observation of laws of nature, e.g., $E=MC^2$, physical phenomena, and abstract idea would be excluded from patentable subject matter. As announced by Judge Linn in *Nuijten*, "the most straightforward interpretation of the Supreme Court's guidance in Chakrabarty is that an invention qualifies as patentable subject matter if it (1) is 'made by man,' and (2) does not involve an attempt to patent "law of nature, physical phenomena, or abstract ideas."[78]

As discussed above, although a signal can be found in nature, e.g., electromagnetic waves, a signal modulated with specific information (e.g., FM radio signals) is not a product of a natural phenomenon. Such signals are man made to be transmitted, to carry specific functions that manifest tangible act, received and demodulated. The modulated signals although transitory are measurable and exist at least for the period of transmission time. Therefore, a signal within the definition offered in this article is not a product or law of nature, a natural phenomenon, or abstract idea. Such a signal is man made and well within the meaning of an article of manufacture as intended by Congress and interpreted by the Supreme Court.

Many aspects of patent law under 35 USC § 101 remain elusive. The USPTO has published several interim guidelines in the last ten years, but these guidelines are forever changing making it difficult for both Examiners and practitioners to gauge the state of the law. This uncertainty also places a cloud on the patent owner's property, which in turn affect the value of these properties. Currently, many issues pertaining to 35 U.S.C. §101 remain unresolved despite the many opinions by the CAFC and numerous interim guidelines published by the USPTO. The eligibility of patented subject matter seems to forever change from eligible patent subject matter one moment to non-eligible patent subject matter the next.[79]

This uncertainty in this area of the law provides an impetus for Congress to step in and enact changes to 35 U.S.C. §101 amending the language of the statute. The Morse's signals of 1853 comprised a fluctuation in electric potential or magnetic fields just as the Nuijten's signals of 2008. The laws of physics have not changed; patent laws however, remain elusive. The two signals exhibit the same characteristics. However, the former enjoyed patentable subject matter status whereas the latter is denied such protection. Hence, there is a need for clarification and direction from Congress.

VIII. CONCLUSION

If the Supreme Court does not take the opportunity to finally settle this issue of scope and interpretation of the statute as it currently reads, this article proposes that Congress codifies *Chakrabarty*. In *Chakrabarty*, the Court observed: "Congress thus recognized that the relevant distinction was not between living and inanimate things, but between products of nature, whether living or not, and human made inventions."[lm3] As articulated above, the uncertainty casts a shadow in this area of the law. We believe it would be proper and indeed prophylactic for Congress to formulate the legislative policies aimed at providing some equilibrium in this area of the law. One way to achieve this objective would be to codify *Chakrabarty*.

The new proposed 35 U.S.C. §101 would thus read:

> Whoever invents or discovers any new and useful human made process, machine, manufacture, composition of matter, or any new and useful improvement thereof, may obtain a patent therefore, subject to the conditions and requirements of this title.

[1]   Albert DeCady holds a Master's Degree in Electrical Engineering from the City College of New York; Masters of Science in Information System from George Washington University and a Juris Doctor from the American University, Washington College of Law. Mr. DeCady is admitted in Maryland and New Jersey. Mr. DeCady is one of the founders of the Haitian-American Intellectual Property Association (HAIPA). Mr. DeCady currently works at the United States Patent and Trademark Office (USPTO) as a Supervisory Patent Examiner. Mr. Decady was an associate at the law firm of Sughrue Mion, PLLC before returning to the USPTO.

[2]   Emmanuel Coffy is an ex–Patent Examiner. Mr. Coffy is an Associate in the IP section of Cozen O'Connor. Mr. Coffy obtained a Master's Degree in Electrical Engineering from Florida Institute of Technology. Mr. Coffy was accepted as a Ph.D. candidate at Stevens Institute. Mr. Coffy graduated from Seton Hall School of Law and is admitted in New Jersey.

[3]   Disclaimer: The authors' opinions discussed herein are solely those of the authors, which should not be attributed to their employers, the USPTO and Cozen O'Connor, or any of its clients.

[4]   Petrus A.C.M. Nuijten v. Jonathan W. Dudas, 500 F.3d 1346 (Fed. Cir. 2007) (en banc reh'g denied February 11, 2008); writ of certiorari filed on May 9, 2008 (Response due August 13, 2008); Nuijten's Brief was filed on Aug. 26, 2008 and is distributed for conference of September 29, 2008; Intellectual Property Academics and American Intellectual Law Association filed Brief amici curiae.

[5]   An electrical wave used to convey information. (Newton's Telecom Dictionary, sixth edition).

[6]   O'Reilly v. Morse, 56 U.S. 62 (1853).

[7]   Gottschalk v. Benson, 409 U.S. 63 (1972).

[8]   Diamond v. Chakrabarty, 447 U.S. 303, 308 (1980).

[9]   Under 35 USC §101: Whoever invents or discovers any new and useful <u>process, machine, manufacture, or composition of matter,</u> or any new and useful improvement thereof, may obtain a patent therefore, subject to the conditions and requirements of this title.

[10] 283 U.S. 1, 11 (1931).

[11] 447 U.S. 303, 308 (1980).

[12] *In Re Nuijten*, 500 F.3d

[13] *Chakrabarty*, 447 U.S.

[14] *Id.*

[15] *Id.*

[16] In the computer industry, technology is perishable and moves faster than in any other industry. This rapid-fire pace means continuous increases in productivity and competitiveness for our industry and the myriad of other industries—from health care and manufacturing to transportation and retail—that have come to depend on computer products and services for their validity. It also means that cutting-edge products are obsolete practically overnight. So, as product life cycles are continually decreasing, the value of quickly bringing products to market is continually increasing. In this dynamic environment, speed is essential. So far, the computer industry has succeeded by using change to its advantage. <u>Every 18 months,</u> advances in technology virtually double the amount of computing power a dollar will buy. *See*http://www.ibiblio.org/darlene/CSPP/CSPP-Technology.

[17] Even when a claim applies a mathematical formula, for example, as part of a seemingly patentable process, however, one must ensure that it does not in reality "seek[] patent protection for that formula in the abstract. *Diamond v. Diehr*, 450 U.S. 175, 191 (1981), 209 USPQ 1, 10 (1981).

[18] *See* Annex II (v) and (vi), USPTO Guidelines, page 16. See United States Patent and Trademark Office: Interim Guidelines for Examination of Patent Applications for Patent Subject Matter Eligibility (Nov. 22, 2005), available at http:// www.uspto.gov/ go/og/2005/week47/patgupa.htm, at page 16.

[19] An electrical wave used to convey information. *Newton's Telecom Dictionary* (6th ed.).

[20] Scott Horstemeyer et al., *A New Frontier in Patents*, 17 J. Marshall J. Computer & Info. L. 75 (1998).

[21] Stephen G. Kunin and Bradley D. Lytle, *Patent Eligibility of Signal Claims*, 87 Journal of the Patent & Trademark Office Society 12.

[22] *See* O'Reilly v. Morse, 56 U.S. 62 (1854). I also claim as my invention the system of signs, consisting of dots and spaces, and of dots, spaces and horizontal lines, substantially as herein set forth and illustrated, in combination with machinery for recording them, as signals for telegraphic purposes.

[23] *See* Kunin, *supra* note 19.

[24] 409 U.S. 63 (1972).

[25] 450 U.S. 175 (1981).

[26] 33 F.3d 1526 (Fed. Cir. 1994).

[27] 32F.3d 1579 (Fed. Cir. 1994).

[28] 53 F.3d 1583 (Fed. Cir. 1995).

[29] United States Patent and Trademark Office: Interim Guidelines for Examination of Patent Applications for Patent Subject Matter Eligibility (Nov. 22, 2005), available at http:// www.uspto.gov/ go/og/2005/week47/patgupa.htm.

[30] While this article pertains to the subject of patentable subject matter as a whole, it only focuses on the issues of signal claims. However, the article also posits that everything made by man (human made) should be included under 35 U.S.C. 101 (as announced in *Diamond v. Chakrabarty*, 447 U.S. 303 (1980)).

[31] No. 2006-1286 (Fed. Cir. Sept. 20, 2007).

[32] *See The Federal Circuit Limits the Scope of Patentable Subject Matter for Mental Processes and Signals*, Foley and Lardner Newsletter (Sep. 28,2007), http://www.foley.com/publications/pub_detail. aspx?pubid=4447

[33] *In re Nuijten*, slip op. at 1.

[34] A petition for rehearing en banc was filed by the Appellant, and a response thereto was invited by the court and filed by the Director of the United States Patent and Trademark Office. The petition for rehearing was referred to the panel that heard the appeal, and thereafter the petition for rehearing en banc and response were referred to the circuit judges who are authorized to request a poll whether to rehear the appeal en banc. A poll was requested, taken, and failed. Petition denied. *In re Nuijten*, 500 F. 3d

[35] *See* Motion Picture Patents Co. v. Universal Film Manufacturing Co., 243 U.S. 502 (1917).

[36] Note that software not considered patentable subject until the decision in *Alappat*. In fact, software by itself is still considered non-statutory subject matter under 35 U.S. C. 101. In view of *Alappat*, a program stored on computer readable media is statutory because the computer readable media fall under the rubric of manufacture.

[37] The permission granted by competent authority to exercise a certain privilege that, without such authorization, would constitute an illegal act, a trespass or a tort. http://legal-dictionary.thefreedictionary.com/license

[38] This problem is similar to the problem confronted by the music industry brought about by the ease of transmitting music via the web. *See A&M Records, Inc. v. Napster, Inc.*, 239 F.3d 1004 (9th Cir. 2001).

[39] *See* Professor Lee A. Hollaar, *Legal Protection of Digital Information.* "In 1998, Congress updated the copyright laws by passing the Digital Millennium Copyright Act (DMCA). In the report that accompanied the Senate version of the bill, the Committee on the Judiciary stated the reasons why Congress needed to act:

Due to the ease with which digital works can be copied and distributed worldwide virtually instantaneously, copyright owners will hesitate to make their works readily available on the Internet without reasonable assurance that they will be protected against massive piracy. Legislation implementing the treaties provides this protection and creates the legal platform for launching the global digital on-line marketplace for copyrighted works. It will facilitate making available quickly and conveniently via the Internet the movies, music, software, and literary works that are the fruit of American creative genius. It will also encourage the continued growth of the existing off-line global marketplace for copyrighted works in digital format by setting strong international copyright standards.

At the same time, without clarification of their liability, service providers may hesitate to make the necessary investment in the expansion of the speed and capacity of the Internet. In the ordinary course of their operations service providers must engage in all kinds of acts that expose them to potential copyright infringement liability. For example, service providers must make innumerable electronic copies by simply transmitting information over the Internet. Certain electronic copies are made to speed up the delivery of information to users. Other electronic copies are made in order to host World Wide Web sites. Many service providers engage in directing users to sites in response to inquiries by users or they volunteer sites that users may find attractive. Some of these sites might contain infringing material. In short, by limiting the liability of service providers, the

DMCA ensures that the efficiency of the Internet will continue to improve and that the variety and quality of services on the Internet will continue to expand. Pub. L 105–304, 112 State. 2860 (Oct. 28, 1998).

[40] In order to be held as a direct infringer of a United States patent under 35 USC § 271(a), it is necessary during the life of the patent to have made, used, offered to sell or sold what is claimed in the patent within the United States or to have imported the patented invention into the United States. *See* http://www.ladas. com/Patents/Biotechnology/USPharmPatentLaw/USPhar27. html.

[41] *See* Kunin, *supra* note 19. "A method patent is not infringed unless the accused process substantially follows the patented method and employs all of the steps or stages of the patented process . . . in such case the infringer is often not the patent holder's competitor but is more often the customer of the patent holder's competitor. The competitor, who is supplying the process claims, would only be liable for contributory infringement. Contributory infringement is defined under 35 U. S. C. 271. To be liable for contributory infringement, the end user must be found liable for direct infringement . . . Many courts require a showing of intent as well . . . [in short] establishing a case of contributory infringement is a significant burden on the patent owner." *Id.*

[42] "A signal produced by a claimed method is broadcast from an offshore location. The signal is received by end users with devices that implement a claimed method. The devices also have significant non–infringing uses. Without a signal claim, the only infringing activity in the U.S. is being done by the individual users." Anonymous, [Post], http://www.patentlyo. com/patent/2008/02/signal–claims–n.html.

[43] A discussion of contributory infringement vs. direct infringement is beyond the scope of this article.

[44] Scott A. Horstemeyer and Daniel J. Santos, *A New Frontier in Patents: Patent Claims to Propagated Signals*, 17 J. Marshall Journal Computer & Info. L. 75 (1998).

[45] The term "literal infringement" means that each and every element recited in a claim has identical correspondence in the allegedly infringing device or process. However, even if there is no literal infringement, a claim may be infringed under the doctrine of equivalents if some other element of the accused device or process performs substantially the same function, in substantially the same way, to achieve substantially the same result. This "expansion" of claim coverage permitted by the doctrine of equivalents, however, is not unbounded. Instead, the scope of coverage which is afforded the patent owner is limited by (i) the doctrine of "prosecution history estoppel" and (ii) the prior art. *See* http://www.intellectual.com/infringement.htm.

[46] "Can someone explain what patentable idea is found in a propagating signal that can't be protected by some statutory non-signal claims?" There isn't any, JTS. But the reason that certain entities care about the patents to the signals is that such patents would allow those entities to file lots of really annoying lawsuits against anyone unfortunate enough to accidentally receive or carry (i.e., "using") the patented signal. Some of the pointy-heads out there who favor signal claims like to pretend that signal patentability is a "scientific issue" but it's really not (nobody subscribes to the view that any signal carrying a novel sound or image is patentable). It's about corporate greed and corrupt telecommunication companies. Lionel Hutz, http://www.patentlyo.com/patent/2008/02/signal-claims-n.html.

[47] IBM, Corporation's Comments on Interim Guidelines for Examination of Patent Subject Matter Eligibility (2006).

[48] *In Re Nuijten,* 500 F.3d.

[49] *Id*. at 15, 18.

[50] *Id*. at 14.

[51] Stephen Hawking, *A Brief History of Time* (1st ed. 1988).

[52] *In Re Nuijten*, 500 F.3d

[53] *Webster's Third New International Dictionary of the English Language Unabridged* 2337 (Philip Babcock ed. 1993).

[54] The majority in *In re Nuijten* states: "While such a transmission is man-made and physical–*it exists in the real world and has tangible causes and effects . . .*" 500 F.3d at (emphasis added).

[55] 447 U.S. at 309–10.

[56] "The watermark Nuijten posits here is imposed on the signal by altering, if necessary, every hundredth value of the digital signal. A reader seeking to extract the watermark from the digital signal would therefore view only every hundredth value, disregarding the other 99 along the way; by stringing together all such values, the watermarked data may be discerned. Every point where a portion of the watermark is found represents a possibility that the signal may be distorted. If the watermark value designated for a certain position and the original value at that same position happen to coincide, there is no need to modify the original and hence no distortion." See Nuijten slip op. at page 4.

[57] Raoul, [Post], http://www.patentlyo.com/patent/2008/02/signal-claims-n.html. "What is the big deal on signal claims? A radio wave, light beam, sound wave, whatever, by itself, is useless. Signals only become interesting or valuable when then make machines do things. A radio wave must be received and handled by circuitry and processes performed by the circuitry. A signal must be produced by some device or process. If the signal is new and non-obvious, mustn't it follow that also new/non-obvious are: the method for producing it, a tangible media storing it, a device for receiving and decoding it, something to generate the signal, you get the idea. Why the fuss over signal claims? Can anyone point to any real world attempt to enforce such a claim (pre-Nuitjen)? With success? Can someone explain what patentable idea is found in a propagating signal that can't

be protected by some statutory non-signal claims? I've written apps for signal processing inventions, inventions about improving features of signals, and I never felt that there was a gap in the various method, system, and media claims. If there's a signal, it's only useful when it's actually received, but at that point you're in statutory territory . . ." *Id.*

[58] Stephen G. Kunin and Bradley D. Lytle, *Patent Eligibility of Signal Claims*, 87 Journal of the Patent & Trademark Office Society.

[59] *See* Professor Lee Hollaar, *ibid.* "Contributory infringement results when somebody knows of the direct infringement of another and substantially participates in that infringement, such as inducing, causing, or materially contributing to the infringing conduct. That substantial participation could take the form of providing a device or service that facilitates the infringement if that device or service has no substantial use other than infringement. In the classic case on contributory infringement, the Supreme Court's 1984 "Betamax" decision. *Id.*, citing *Sony v. Universal City Studios*, 464 U.S. 417, 220 USPQ 665 (1984) (the Court held that Sony was not a contributory infringer by selling VCRs because there was a number of uses for the VCR (including time-shifting of a broadcast program for personal use) that would not infringe copyright).

[60] *Id.* "Vicarious infringement results when there has been a direct infringement and the vicarious infringer is in a position to control the direct infringer and benefits financially from the infringement. In a 1996 Ninth Circuit case, citing *Fonovisa Inc. v. Cherry Auction*, 76 F.3d 259, 37 USPQ2d 1590 (9th Cir. 1996), the operator of a flea market where counterfeit recordings were regularly sold was found to be a vicarious infringer because he could have policed the vendors who rented booths from him but didn't, and he made money from that booth rental as well as from admission fees from the people attending the flea market. The court believed that many of the people who paid those admission fees did so to gain access to the counterfeit recordings. The court also found that the flea market operator was guilty of contributory infringement.

[61] *See* IBM, *supra* note 45 [check once footnote numbers finalized].

[62] *See* Sam Han, [Post], http://www.patentlyo.com/ patent/2008/02/signal-claims-n.html. "Merely by way of example, the DMCA found it necessary to include a safe harbor position for "signals" coursing over the internet. It is by no means a stretch of the imagination to consider that the grant of a patent for Nuijten's "signal" could raise significant tension between copyright and patent law on an issue that has been considered by Congress, albeit in the context of copyright law. Of course, for now the rule is "signals are out" unless Nuijten petitions for cert and the SCOTUS once more decides the time is ripe to revisit 101. Personally, I happen to like these facts as a vehicle for revisiting the issue precisely because they push the envelope of conventional wisdom. It would certainly help to clarify in my mind if the reach of 101 will continue to be determined incrementally by the judiciary or by referral to Congress. Jurisprudence concerning 101 has been a slave to words crafted in the 1700's. Innovation is rapidly moving into areas that not too long ago were never even envisioned. How nice it would be to see those "words" brought up to date to reflect technological reality." *Id.*

[63] *See Graham v. John Deere Co.*, 383 U.S. 1, 7–10, 148 USPQ 459, 462–464 (1966).

[64] *Corning,* 56 U.S. (15 How.) at 268, 14 L.Ed. 683.

[65] The statute was amended in 1790, 1793, 1800, 1870 prior to this version. *See* Sam S. Han, PhD, *Analyzing the Patentability of 'Intangible" yet 'Physical' Subject Matter.*

[66] *Id.*at *History of the Patent Statutes.* "Although not all of the original Patent Act of 1970 deals with patentable subject matter, it is worthwhile to examine, at a minimum, the first paragraph of the statute and compare it with the constitutional text. The First Congress enacted the Patent Act of 1790, which provided:

That upon the petition of any person or persons to the Secretary of State, the Secretary for the department of war, and the Attorney General of the United States, setting forth, that he, she, or they, hath or have invented or discovered any useful art, manufacture, engine, machine, or device, or any improvement therein not before known or used, and praying that a patent may be granted therefore, it shall and may be lawful to and for the said Secretary of State, the Secretary for the department of war, and the Attorney General, or any two of them, if they shall deem the invention or discovery sufficiently useful and important, to cause letters patent to be made out in the name of the United States, or to bear teste by the president of the United States, reciting the allegations and suggestions of the said petition, and describing the said invention or discovery, clearly, truly and fully, and thereupon granting to such petitioner or petitioners, his, her or their heirs, administrators or assigns for any term not exceeding fourteen years, the sole and exclusive right and liberty of making, constructing, using and vending to others to be use, the said invention or discovery . . .

In 1793, Congress amended the Patent Act to read:

That when any person or persons, being a citizen or citizens of the United States, shall allege that he or they have discovered any new and useful art, machine, manufacture or composition of matter, or any new and useful improvement on any art, machine, manufacture or composition of matter, not known or used before the application, and shall present a petition to the Secretary of State, signifying a desire of obtaining an exclusive property in the same, and praying that a patent may be granted therefor, it shall and may be lawful for the said Secretary of State, to cause letters patent to be made out in the name of the United States, bearing teste by the President of the United States, reciting the allegations and suggestions of the said petition, and giving a short description of the said invention or discovery, and thereupon granting to such petitioner, or petitioners, his, her, or their heirs, Administrators or assigns, for a term not exceeding fourteen years, the full and exclusive right and liberty of making constructing, using, and vending to others to be used, the said invention or discovery, which letters patent shall be delivered to the Attorney General of the United States, to be examined . . . The two most significant textual changes with respect to patentability were (1) the change in subject matter categories, and (2) the change in the disclosure requirement . . . In the subject matter categories, "art, manufacture, engine, machine, or device" . . . was amended to "art, machine, manufacture or composition of matter . . . It is unclear whether this amendment reduced the scope of patentable subject matter by reducing the categories of allowable subject matter, or whether the amendment merely collapsed duplicate categories and maintained the scope of patentable subject matter . . .

The next amendment, made in 1800, neither added nor subtracted significantly from the amendment of 1794. The Patent Act was further amended in 1836 to read:

That any person or persons having discovered or invented any new and useful art, machine, manufacture, or composition of matter, or any new and useful improvement on any art, machine, manufacture, or composition of matter, not known or used by others before his or their discovery or invention thereof, and not, at the time of his application for a patent, in public use or on sale, with his consent or allowance, as the inventor or discoverer; and shall desire to obtain an exclusive property therein, may make application in writing to the Commissioner of Patents, expressing such desire, and the Commissioner, on due proceedings had, may grant a patent therefor.

While the wording of the statute changed, it appears that little changed with respect to patentable subject matter. The categories remained "art, machine, manufacture, or composition of matter[,]" and was still limited to "new and useful" subject matter. Much of the language was simplified in 1870 to read:

That any person who has invented or discovered any new and useful art, machine, manufacture, or composition of matter, or any new and useful improvement thereof, not known or used by others in this country, and not patented, or described in any printed publication in this or any foreign country, before his invention or discovery thereof, and not in public use or on sale for more than two years prior to his application, unless the same is proved to have been abandoned, may, upon payment of the duty required by law, and other due proceedings had, obtain a patent therefor.

Despite several changes in the statute with respect to previously published material, not much changed in the way of the categories of patentable subject matter (i.e., "art, machine, manufacture, or composition of matter") or the novelty and usefulness requirements (i.e., "new and useful"). This language remained virtually unchanged in subsequent amendments and, in 1952, crystallized to the current patent statute, 35 U.S.C. § 101, which provides:

Whoever invents or discovers any new and useful process, machine, manufacture, or composition of matter, or any new and useful improvement thereof, may obtain a patent therefor, subject to the conditions and requirements of this title.

[67] *See* 35 U.S.C. §§102 and 103.

35 U.S.C. 102 states: A person shall be entitled to a patent unless—

(a) the invention was known or used by others in this country, or patented or described in a printed publication in this or a foreign country, before the invention thereof by the applicant for patent, or

(b) the invention was patented or described in a printed publication in this or a foreign country or in public use or on sale in this country, more than one year prior to the date of the application for patent in the United States, or

(c) he has abandoned the invention, or

(d) the invention was first patented or caused to be patented, or was the subject of an inventor's certificate, by the applicant or his legal representatives or assigns in a foreign country prior to the date of the application for patent in this country on an application for patent or inventor's certificate filed more than twelve months before the filing of the application in the United States, or

(e) the invention was described in—(1) an application for patent, published under section 122(b), by another filed in the United States before the invention by the applicant for patent or (2) a patent granted on an application for patent by another filed in the United States before the invention by the applicant for patent, except that an international application filed under the treaty defined in section 351(a) shall have the effects for the purposes of this subsection of an application filed in the United States only if the international application designated the United States and was published under Article 21(2) of such treaty in the English language; or

(f) he did not himself invent the subject matter sought to be patented, or

(g) (1) during the course of an interference conducted under section 135 or section 291, another inventor involved therein establishes, to the extent permitted in section 104, that before such person's invention thereof the invention was made by such other inventor and not abandoned, suppressed, or concealed, or (2) before such person's invention thereof, the invention was made in this country by another inventor who had not abandoned, suppressed, or concealed it. In determining priority of invention under this subsection, there shall be considered not only the respective dates of conception and reduction to practice of the invention, but also the reasonable diligence of one who was first to conceive and last to reduce to practice, from a time prior to conception by the other.

35 U.S.C. 103 states:

A patent may not be obtained though the invention is not identically disclosed or described as set forth in section 102 of this title, if the differences between the subject matter sought to be patented and the prior art are such that the subject matter as a whole would have been obvious at the time the invention was made to a person having ordinary skill in the art to which said subject matter pertains. Patentability shall not be negatived by the manner in which the invention was made.

(1) Notwithstanding subsection (a), and upon timely election by the applicant for patent to proceed under this subsection, a biotechnological process using or resulting in a composition of matter that is novel under section 102and nonobvious under subsection (a) of this section shall be considered nonobvious if—

(A) claims to the process and the composition of matter are contained in either the same application for patent or in separate applications having the same effective filing date; and

(B) the composition of matter, and the process at the time it was invented, were owned by the same person or subject to an obligation of assignment to the same person.

(2) A patent issued on a process under paragraph (1)—

(A) shall also contain the claims to the composition of matter used in or made by that process, or

(B) shall, if such composition of matter is claimed in another patent, be set to expire on the same date as such other patent, notwithstanding section 154.

(3) For purposes of paragraph (1), the term "biotechnological process" means—

(A) a process of genetically altering or otherwise inducing a single- or multi-celled organism to—

(i) express an exogenous nucleotide sequence,

(ii) inhibit, eliminate, augment, or alter expression of an endogenous nucleotide sequence, or

(iii) express a specific physiological characteristic not naturally associated with said organism;

(B) cell fusion procedures yielding a cell line that expresses a specific protein, such as a monoclonal antibody; and

(C) a method of using a product produced by a process defined by subparagraph (A) or (B), or a combination of subparagraphs (A) and (B).

(1) Subject matter developed by another person, which qualifies as prior art only under one or more of subsections (e), (f), and (g) of section 102 of this title, shall not preclude patentability under this section where the subject matter and the claimed invention were, at the time the claimed invention was made, owned by the same person or subject to an obligation of assignment to the same person.

(2) For purposes of this subsection, subject matter developed by another person and a claimed invention shall be deemed to have been owned by the same person or subject to an obligation of assignment to the same person if—

(A) the claimed invention was made by or on behalf of parties to a joint research agreement that was in effect on or before the date the claimed invention was made;

(B) the claimed invention was made as a result of activities undertaken within the scope of the joint research agreement; and

(C) the application for patent for the claimed invention discloses or is amended to disclose the names of the parties to the joint research agreement.

(3) For purposes of paragraph (2), the term "joint research agreement" means a written contract, grant, or cooperative

agreement entered into by two or more persons or entities for the performance of experimental, developmental, or research work in the field of the claimed invention.

[68] *Ibid*, at page 4.

[69] *Id*. In *In re Musgrave*, the CCPA [predecessor court to the CAFC] seemed to establish a new 'technological arts' standard for determining patentable subject matter, thus broadening the scope of patentable subject matter to encompass almost anything . . . The Supreme Court, however, significantly curtailed the scope of patentable subject matter in *Gottschalk v. Benson*. In invalidating a method patent for converting binary-coded decimal numbers to pure binary numbers as being nothing more than a patent on a mathematical algorithm, the Court reiterated the policy from *O'Reilly*, that the public must not be deprived of the laws of nature. The Court reasoned that, since algorithms (i.e., laws of nature) were not directly patentable because it would deprive the public of "[a] basic tool of scientific and technological work[,]" indirect patenting of algorithms should be disallowed since indirect patenting of algorithms would also defeat this policy. Thus, the Supreme Court seemed to apply the same analysis to Benson (i.e., mere programming of an algorithm into a computer is insufficient to confer statutory status to nonstatutory subject matter) as it did to Greater Atlantic & Pacific Tea Co. (i.e., mere skill was insufficient to transform unpatentable subject matter into patentable subject matter). The CCPA, however, continued to resist narrowing the scope of patentable subject matter and, instead, narrowed the holding of Benson in subsequent cases.

[70] *In Re Nuijten*, 500 F. 3d. at Dissent.

[71] *See* 35 U.S.C. §§101, 102, 103, 112.

[72] *See* KSR Int'l Co. v. Teleflex Inc., 127 S.Ct. 1727, 1734 (Section 103 forbids issuance of a patent when 'the differences between the subject matter sought to be patented and the prior art are such that the subject matter as a whole would have been obvious at the time of the invention was made to a person of ordinary

skill in the art to which said subject matter pertains' . . . the combination of familiar elements according to known methods is likely to be obvious when it does no more than yield predictable results.) In *KSR*, the Court announced other factors that may be considered in refusing a patent: Common sense, obvious to try, official notice, design choice . . .

[73] "A signal that is specially shaped by man is not a naturally occurring phenomenon but rather something made by man under the sun. The issue should be whether it is novel and useful, not whether its inventor is not to be allowed to stick his toe into the Patent Office door." Ironicslip, [Post], http://www.patentlyo. com/patent/2008/02/signal-claims-n.html.

[74] 447 U.S. at 308–09.

[75] *See* USPTO, *supra* note, at Eligibility, Section IV(A).

[76] 447 U.S.

[77] *See In Re Nuijten*, 500 F. 3d. at 10, *citing Chakrabarty, 447 U.S.*at 309 (*quoting* S. Rep. No. 82-1979, at 5 (1952); H.R. Rep. No. 82-1923, at 6 (1952)).

[78] *Id.*

[79] There are several decisions on the matter, but none established a bright line of what is patentable under §101. Several issues are now pending decision at CAFC. *See, e.g., In re Bilski,* 2008 WL 417680 (Fed. Cir. 2008) (oral arguments heard en banc May 8, 2008; *In re Ferguson,* No. 2007-1232 (Fed. Cir. 2007), (oral arguments heard December 5, 2007). Both are still awaiting the CAFC's decision. These decisions by the CAFC are predicted to narrow the scope of 35 U.S.C. 101. A further narrowing of 35 U.S.C. 101 would make many issued patented claims unenforceable, many pending patent application worthless, and potentially could eliminate whole classes or subclasses for many years that were considered eligible for patent. [lm1]It appears the citation to the federal reporter is now available, 500 F.3d 1346 (Fed. Cir. 2007).

APPENDIX B

LIST OF CERTAIN ORGANIZATIONS FOR INVENTORS

1. Alabama – Invent Alabama (866)745-6319
    i. Alabama Inventors Clubs (256) 229-5551
    ii. Columbus Phenix City Inventors Association (www.cpcinventorsassociation.weebly.com)
2. Alaska – Alaska Inventors & Entrepreneurs Inventors Institute of Alaska (907) 376-5114
3. Arizona – Inventors Association of Arizona, Inc. (www.azinventors.org)
    i. TechShop Inventors Club (602) 303-6272
4. Arkansas – arkansasinvents.org
5. California - Inventors Alliance (www.inventorsalliance.org)
    i. Inventors Forum (inventorsforum.org)
    ii. San Diego Inventors Forum (www.sdinventors.org)
    iii. Thomas Jefferson School of Law Patent Clinic
6. Colorado – Rocky Mountain Inventors association (www.rminventor.org)
7. Connecticut Invention Convention (www.ctinventionconvention.org)
8. Delaware Entrepreneurs Forum (302) 652-4241
9. District of Columbia – Inventors Network of the Capital Area (www.dcinventors.org)
10. Florida – Edison Inventors Association, Inc. (www.edisoninventors.org)
11. Tampa Bay Inventors' Council (www.tbic.us)

12. Inventors Society of South Florida (www.inventorssociety.net)
13. Georgia – Inventors Association of Georgia, Inc. (www. GAInventors.org)
14. Hawaii International Inventors Association, Inc. (808) 523-5555
15. Idaho – Inventors Association of Idaho (208) 255-4131 x223 (www.inventorsassociationofidaho.com)
     i. East Idaho Inventors Forum (208) 346-6763
16. Illinois Innovators and Inventors (www.ilinventor.tripod.com)
     i. Chicago Inventors Organization (www. chicago-inventors.org)
     ii. INVINT – Central Illinois Innovation Viability Network (www.invint.org)
17. Indiana Inventors association – (765-674-2845) Inventors Council-Wabash (219) 782-2511
18. Iowa Inventors Group (iowainventorsgroup.org)
19. Drake University Inventor Program (515) 271-2655
20. Inventors Association of So. Central Kansas (316) 681-2358
     i. Mid-America Inventors Association (913) 371-7011
     ii. Inventor's Club of KC (www. inventorsclubofkc.org)
21. Central Kentucky Inventors Council (www.ckic.org)
22. Inventors Network of the Capital Area (www.dcinventors.org)
23. Inventors' Association of New England (www.inventne.org)
     i. Inventors' Roundtable (www. inventorsrountable.com)
     ii. National Collegiate Inventors & Innovators Alliance (www.nciia.org)
24. The Entrepreneur Network (www.teonline.org)
     i. Inventors Council of Mid Michigan (www. inventorscouncil.org)
     ii. InventorEd.org (www.inventored.org)
     iii. The Flint and Genesee Regional Chamber of Commerce (www.thegrcc.org)
25. Inventors' Network (www.inventornetwork.org)
     i. Minnesota Inventors Congress (www. minnesotainventorscongress.org)
26. Society of Mississippi Inventors Assistance (www.mssbdc.org)

27. Inventors Association of St. Louis (www.inventorsconnection.org)
28. Montana Inventors Association (406) 586-1541 – Blue Sky Inventors (406)
29. Lincoln Inventors Association
30. Nevada Inventors Association (www.nevadainventors.org)
31. New Hampshire Inventors (603) 228-3854
32. National Society of Inventors (609) 799-4574 (www.nationalinventors.com)
    i. New Jersey Entrepreneurs Forum (www.njef.org)
33. New Mexico Inventors Club (505) 266-3541
34. Inventors Society of Western New York (www.inventny.org)
    i. Suffolk County Inventors and Entrepreneurs Club (631) 415-5013
    ii. Inventors Association of Manhattan (www.manhattan-inventors.org)
35. Inventors' Network of the Carolinas (www.inotc.org)
36. Northern Plains Inventors Congress (www.ndinventors.com) (701) 281-8822
37. Inventors Connection Greater Cleveland (440) 941-6567
    i. Inventor's Council of Cincinnati (www.inventcincy.org)
38. Oklahoma Inventors Congress (www.oklahomainventors.com) (405) 348-7794
39. Portland Inventors Group (503) 288-4558
    i. Micro-Inventors Program of Oregon (www.mipooregon.org)
    ii. South Oregon Inventors Council (541) 772-3478
40. American Society of Inventors (www.americaninventor.org)
    i. Pittsburgh East Inventors Club (www.inventionburgh.wordpress.com)
41. The Center for Design & Business (401) 454-6108
42. Inventors Network of the Carolinas (www.portal.inotc.org)
43. South Dakota Inventors Congress (605) 688-4184
44. Inventors' Association of Middle Tennessee (615) 681-6462
    i. Tennessee Inventors Association (www.tninventors.org)

45. Alamo Inventors (www.alamoinventors.org)
      i. Houston Inventors Association (www.inventors.org)
      ii. Austin Inventors and Entrepreneurs Association (www.austininventors.org)
      iii. Texas Inventors Association (www.txinventors.com)
      iv. Young Inventors Showcase (Houston) (www.younginventorsshowcase.org)
46. Inventors' Roundtable (www.inventorsroundtable.com)
      i. Utah Inventors (utahinventor.org)
47. Invent Vermont (www.inventvermont.com)
48. Inventors Network of the Capital Area (www.dcinventors.org)
      i. Virginia Inventors Forum, Inc. (www.virginianinventors.org)
      ii. Inventors Network (503) 239-8299
49. Inventors Network (503) 239-8299
50. West Virginia Inventors Council Inc. (304) 293-3612 x3730
51. Inventors Network of Wisconsin (920) 429-0331
52. USPTO National Council for Expanding American Innovation

APPENDIX C

RESOURCES

1. Check out the United State Patent and Trademark site if you want to get a patent and/or a trademark: www.uspto.gov
2. To register your copyright: https://www.copyright.gov/registration/
3. For Korea: https://www.kipo.go.kr/en/MainApp?c=1000
4. For Japan: https://www.jpo.go.jp/e/
5. For China: http://english.sipo.gov.cn
6. The European Patent Office: https://www.epo.org
7. For Africa: https://www.aripo.org
8. For Canada: https://www.ic.gc.ca/eic/site/cipointernet-internetopic.nsf/eng/h_wr00001.html
9. For Australia: https://www.ipaustralia.gov.au
10. For Nigeria: http://www.iponigeria.com/#/
11. For World Intellectual Property Organization: https://www.wipo.int/portal/en/index.html
12. For India: http://www.ipindia.nic.in
13. Google Patent: https://patents.google.com
14. Manual patent examination procedures: https://www.uspto.gov/patent/laws-regulations-policies-procedures-guidance-and-training
15. For Brazil: http://www.inpi.gov.br/english
16. For United Kingdom: https://www.gov.uk/government/organisations/intellectual-property-office
17. For Mexico: https://www.gob.mx/impi

18. Find a registered agent in the United States: https://www.uspto.gov/learning-and-resources/patent-and-trademark-practitioners
19. Federal Trade Commission (FTC): www.ftc.gov
20. Russian Patent Office: www.rupto.ru

APPENDIX D

US GOVERNMENT AGENCIES

These federal agencies are responsible for protecting and enforcing intellectual property rights and preventing counterfeits and pirated goods from entering the market.

- Federal Bureau of Investigation (FBI)
- Federal Trade Commission (FTC)
- Food and Drug Administration (FDA)
- National Intellectual Property Rights Coordination Center
- Office of the United States Trade Representative
- US Department of Commerce
  - Office of Standards and Intellectual Property
  - US Commercial Service
  - US Patent and Trademark Office (USPTO)
- US Consumer Product Safety Commission
- US Copyright Office
- US Customs and Border Protection (CBP)
- US Department of Justice, Computer Crime Initiative
- US Department of State, International Intellectual Property Enforcement
- US Immigration and Customs Enforcement (ICE) and US Homeland Security Investigations (HSI)
- US Intellectual Property Enforcement Coordinator (IPEC)
- US International Trade Commission

INDEX

A

Africans, xv
American Inventors Protection Act (AIPA), 25
ancient civilizations, xvi–xix
artificial intelligence (AI), xx, 69, 76, 80
    machine learning (ML), 76, 80–82
    symbolic learning (SL), 80–81
attorneys, 41, 52, 55, 59–61, 89

B

Berne Convention, 35
blockchain, 85–86

C

civilization, Roman, xix
cloud computing, 45–46
commercialization, 16
competitive advantage valuation (CAV), 66
copyright, 33–34, 56
copyright protection, 34
Court of Appeals for the Federal Circuit (CAFC), 82
crowdfunding, 11
cryptocurrencies, 85

D

Dahl, Gary, 4
Defend Trade Secrets Act (DTSA), 40

D

distribution agreement, 13
domain, 43–44
domain names, 43–44
    top-level, 44

E

e-commerce, 44–45
European Patent Office, 82

F

Federal Trade Commission (FTC), 45
franchising, 13

H

history, xv

I

ideas, 1, 5–6
    failed, 3
    owned by another, 7–8
    protecting, 8–9
influencers
    Instagram, 37
    micro, 37–38
innovation, 49, 56, 72, 77, 80
intellectual property (IP), xiii, 12, 17, 19–20, 47, 61, 70
    categories of, 18
    and courts, 71–73
    definition of, 17
    evolution of, 18
    monetizing, 67

rights, 12, 71
sale of, 15
securing, 51
theft, 72
types of, 20
valuing, 63–64, 66
intellectual property (IP) management, 68–70
internet, 43, 45
Internet Corporation for Assigned Names and Numbers (ICANN), 43
inventions, xx, 77, 79–86
ancient, xvi–xx
moonwalk, 2
nanotechnology, 84
quantum computing, 82–83
teleportation, 84
that shaped 2010, 75–77
websites, 43

J

Jackson, Michael, 2
joint venture, 14

K

Kardashian, Kim, 4–5
Kearns, Robert, 2–3

L

learning, statistical, 81
license, 14
types of, 14

M

marks
certification, 29
common-law, 28
family of, 29–30
Marrakesh Treaty, 35

P

patent agents, 60
Patent Cooperation Treaty (PCT), 55–57
patent laws, 18, 25–26, 52, 54
patent protection, 56
patents, 8, 23–24
types of, 25

R

register
principal, 27, 30–32
supplemental, 31
Rights of Publicity (ROP), 35

S

sales representative, 13
Silver, Spencer, 3
startup, idea-stage, 9–11
success, 11, 16

T

technology, 79
computer, 82
future, 87
and law, 86
quantum, 83–84
technology sale, 15
trade dress, 20, 31–32
trademark rights, 27–28, 48
trademarks, 27, 56
international, 32
types of, 28–29
trade secrets, ix, 12, 20, 39–40, 72
protecting, 40
traditional knowledge (TK), 18, 21, 47–50

U

United States Patent and Trademark Office (USPTO), 51–53

V

valuation, 66
    methods of, 63–66

W

web-hosting services, 44

White, Vanna, 4, 35–36
    case of, 4, 35–36
World Intellectual Property Organization (WIPO), 47, 49, 56, 63
world patent system, 54–55

Printed in the United States
By Bookmasters